CLOSER

CLO

JIM & CATHY BURNS

SER

Cover design by Lookout Design, Inc.

Published by Bethany House Publishers
11400 Hampshire Avenue South
Bloomington, Minnesota 55438

Bethany House Publishers is a division of
Baker Publishing Group, Grand Rapids, Michigan.

Printed in the United States of America

In keeping with biblical principles of creation stewardship, Baker Publishing Group advocates the responsible use of our natural resources. As a member of the Green Press Initiative, our company uses recycled paper when possible. The text paper of this book is comprised of 30% post-consumer waste.

Library of Congress Cataloging-in-Publication Data

Burns, Jim.
Closer: devotions to draw couples together / Jim & Cathy Burns.
p. cm.
Includes biblographical references.
Summary: "Fifty-two devotional readings are presented to help husbands and wives draw closer to God and each other. Includes Bible verses, personal stories, questions to inspire faith-related conversations, and action steps"—Provided by publisher.
ISBN 978-0-7642-0703-7 (hardcover : alk. paper) 1. Marriage. 2. Marriage—Religious aspects. 3. Spouses—Psychology. I. Burns, Cathy. II. Title.
HQ734.B9245 2009
242'.644—dc22

2009025230

To Randy and Susan Bramel

You have touched our lives in so many different ways. Thank you for your friendship, mentoring, and passion for the mission.

Books by

Jim Burns

FROM BETHANY HOUSE PUBLISHERS

Accept Nothing Less

Closer (with Cathy Burns)

*Confident Parenting**

*Creating an Intimate Marriage**

God Made Your Body

How God Makes Babies

The Purity Code

Teaching Your Children Healthy Sexuality†

*Audio CD; DVD & Curriculum Kit also available

†Parents' Kit also available: *The Purity Code, Teaching Your Children Healthy Sexuality,* and special Audio Resource CD

ACKNOWLEDGMENTS

Thank you

Christy, Rebecca, and Heidi . . . You view an imperfect marriage up-close and personal. If we can make it, you can. We are proud of who you are and who you are becoming.

Cindy Ward . . . You are a partner in the mission and an amazing source of encouragement.

The HomeWord Staff . . . You work so hard to serve families. Your efforts have eternal value.

Jon Wallace, David Peck, and Dave Bixby . . . The HomeWord Center for Youth and Family at Azusa Pacific University is a dream come true. We are grateful for your friendships and partnership.

Karen and Dale Walters, Pam and Craig Alexander, Jill and Glen Corey . . . The role you play in our family as godparents is one of our greatest sources of joy and support. We are deeply grateful.

Kyle Duncan, Greg Johnson, and Jeff Braun . . . You are more friends than publishers. The grace you showed us during this season of writing this book has been a gift from God. What a privilege it is to work alongside you to bring messages of hope and healing.

CONTENTS

INTRODUCTION

Over the past thirty years we have tried almost every marriage devotional, and to be perfectly honest, we have usually failed at having the discipline to continue. The busyness of life or the feelings of guilt because we missed so many days often caused us to silently ignore what we knew was important for our growth. This book is the result of our trying to draw closer to each other while having a true desire to improve our spiritual growth as a couple.

We have friends who read the entire Bible together and others who have an extended time with God together every day. That's not us. We try to pray together almost every day, and we've settled on a weekly time for further spiritual connection. If you are farther along the road than us, this book may not work for you; or you can power through it in fifty-two days instead of fifty-two weeks. Our challenge to couples is to start small and invest thirty minutes a week. That may sound wimpy, but we figure something is better than nothing, and that's exactly what most people settle for: nothing.

Closer is meant to be done together whenever possible. Each reading starts with a Scripture and a story or main point relating to a theme in your life and marriage. We kept the Scripture and body of the devotional short because we have found the best way to go through a devotional for couples is to read it together. The most effective and impactful part of each devotional might not be in the words we wrote but rather the "Faith Conversations" and "A Step Closer" dialogues you and your spouse can have after you have read the words together. We have found that we learn best when we talk about the important topics related to our marriage, and that without directed communication, we can easily slack off and move toward shallowness.

We challenge couples wherever we go to invest a set amount of time each week to come together to be inspired, communicate, and pray together. Our experience is that we have never met a couple who has gotten a divorce after praying together daily and having a spiritual growth time at least once a week. Perhaps the least developed part of most relationships is spiritual growth. For some, it's too overwhelming. For others, it might be that they can't connect because there is tension or anger. We find that regardless of how you are feeling about each other, setting apart a regular time to focus on the practical side of your spiritual life will do wonders for your relationship. Actually, over the years we have seen miraculous results when couples take the challenge to grow together spiritually. The result we hear most often is that they grew *closer* to God and *closer* to each other.

So here's the deal. We want to challenge you to a weekly time together to focus on your spiritual life as a couple. If you miss a week, don't quit—just pick up where you left off. This opportunity for togetherness is not about a legalistic time; it's about setting a priority for practical spiritual growth and connection. Take the challenge! Some of the devotionals will be more meaningful to you than others, but just keep on keeping on. These Scriptures, stories, and observations are some of our favorites. The discussion topics have brought about great times of connection and even a few tears or tension. But the net result has been a drawing closer together. This challenge will take some discipline and willingness on your part to draw near to God and to each other. These two verses make a lot of sense to us: "Draw near to God and He will draw near to you" (James 4:8 NASB), as well as Paul's advice to Timothy, "Discipline yourself for the purpose of godliness" (1 Timothy 4:7 NASB). With these thoughts in mind, we hope you will find the closeness, intimacy, and connection that is available to those who seek it and put these words into practice. When you have finished going through this devotional together, let us know how it worked for you. We would love to hear your story.

Blessings,

Jim and Cathy Burns
Dana Point, California
Closer@HomeWord.com

Trusting the Author of Your Story

Trust in the Lord with all your heart and lean not on your own understanding; in all your ways acknowledge him, and he will make your paths straight.

—Proverbs 3:5–6

What is the story of your courtship and marriage? Has God been present from the start? We think he was, no matter if you recognized it at the time or not. Some couples meet under extraordinary experiences that can happen only through God. Our neighbors met and married in a Japanese internment camp during World War II. When they died some sixty years later, it was within twenty-four hours of each other. Jim's parents met on a blind double date in which his mom actually thought she was dating the other guy, not his dad. Walt and Barb Larimore met in the playground sandbox at their church at age five. They are the only love each has ever known. Todd and Becky both lost their spouses early in their marriages. Todd's wife died of a brain tumor and Becky's husband was killed in a skiing accident. Together they have blended their families and their lives. Both would say in the midst of their sorrow, God also brought them joy.

We met on our first day of college and were "just friends" before we started dating. As we look back, it's pretty random that two kids from different parts of California chose the same university, had classes together, and found common friends with common goals. After a couple of breakups with a few starts and stops through college, we married one week after graduation. Of course, hindsight is much easier than foresight, but as we look back, God was present.

What is the story of your relationship? How do you see your early days, as well as today? Plagued with infertility, we look at each of our children as miracles from God. We had to learn to trust in Him. There have been times of sickness, and times where dreams came true and dreams were taken away. There have been career changes and moves to other cities. Hopes appeared and promises were broken. But through it all, God was and is present. There is really nothing all that spectacular about our marriage, but every time we take a deeper look at our life together, one word pops up: miracle. Without God's presence, comfort, prodding, and guidance we don't think we would have made it. Even during the times when we didn't know He was carrying us, He was and is still doing it today.

"Trust in the Lord with all your heart." These are great words but not always easy to do. They mean that no matter what happens, place your life and marriage into the loving arms of God. Your hope and your faith can rest in God's assurance that He will never leave you or forsake you. And that is quite a promise. So, what do you need to completely trust God with right now?

"Lean not on your own understanding." Some people have called belief in God a crutch. We think of it more as an iron lung. Every couple has a choice to lean on God and not their own understanding. We hope today you will choose God. He definitely knows a lot more about life and relationships than any of us. You may not always know exactly where He is taking you, but wouldn't you rather have the God who created the universe actively guide your life and marriage than, well, you? Is there something going on in your life right now where you just don't understand what's happening? In what areas of your life do you need God's presence?

"In all your ways acknowledge him." Today permit God to be involved in your daily activities and relationships. Jesus said it so well in the Sermon on the Mount: "Seek first his kingdom and his righteousness, and all these things [all that we need] will be given to you as well" (Matthew 6:33). It is pretty incredible to watch couples move from doing life on their own to acknowledging God in their decisions. As one couple we know said, "As we sought God's help and intervention, it just seemed to all fall together." That's the point! Where do you need to acknowledge Him today?

"He will make your paths straight." What a wonderful promise! God doesn't promise the path will not be difficult at times, but He does promise—as we put our trust in Him and not do things on our own—that He will guide us. How incredible to look back on our life and marriage and say, God was here.

FAITH CONVERSATIONS

- Courtship and marriage are different for everyone. Let's talk about where we see God in our story.

- The Bible says to trust in the Lord with all your heart and he will direct your path. What does this promise mean to us as a couple?
- Here is how you can help me put my trust in the Lord's guidance more often: ______________________. How can I help you?

A STEP CLOSER

YOUR STORY

Together write out the story of your relationship. How did you meet? What was it that you saw in each other that made you fall in love? What have been high points in your relationship? Low points? If you have children, gather them around you one evening and read your story to them.

Don't Lose Sight of the Goal

I press on toward the goal to win the prize for which God has called me heavenward in Christ Jesus.

—Philippians 3:14

We live in a beautiful beach town, Dana Point, on the coast of Southern California. We never tire of the view. On most days when we are near the water, we see Catalina Island, twenty-six miles offshore. There are a few days when it is foggy and you can't see it, but it is forever etched in our minds. People board boats from the harbor in our town to visit this magical island every day of the year. Some people take a fifteen-minute helicopter flight. A few brave souls paddleboard to the island, but very few ever try to swim there.

In 1952, Florence Chadwick decided to swim from Catalina Island to the shores of Southern California. She had already swum the English Channel, so in her mind, this would be easier. She jumped in the water one cold day in winter. No problem for Florence Chadwick.

But as she swam hour after hour with a boat following her to make sure she was all right, fog settled in and she began to wonder how much farther she had to go. At last she motioned for the boat to pick her up. As it turned out, Florence was only a half mile from reaching her goal. She wasn't too exhausted or cold. The fog had simply obscured her vision from her target. So she quit.

On the day of our wedding we had a goal: to draw closer to each other and closer to God. Too many times, though, the weight of home responsibilities, work pressures, kid worries, and all the rest fog our vision for closeness. Spiritually speaking, everyone has foggy days. But God is there to say to us in His quiet, persistent voice, *"Don't quit. Persevere. Do all you can to keep your eyes focused on the prize."*

The writer of Hebrews gave us a formula for perseverance: "Therefore, since we are surrounded by such a great cloud of witnesses, let us throw off everything that hinders and the sin that so easily entangles, and let us run with perseverance the race marked out for us. Let us fix our eyes on Jesus, the author and perfecter of our faith, who for the joy set before him endured the cross, scorning its shame, and sat down at the right hand of the throne of God. Consider him who endured such opposition from sinful men, so that you will not grow weary and lose heart" (12:1–3). The way not to grow weary and lose heart in your marriage is to keep your eye on the goal. Stay focused on Jesus, our goal, our sustainer, our Savior.

FAITH CONVERSATIONS

- Has there been a time when fog surrounded our marriage?
- What areas of our lives do we need to persevere in right now?
- How can I help you do that?

A STEP CLOSER

GOALS FOR OUR MARRIAGE

Together come up with three goals for your marriage relationship to work on in the next month and list them below. Then think of three action steps that would help you accomplish those goals. Now circle what you can work on *this week*.

1. Hugs, Kisses, Smiles, + I Love You's

2. Being Prayerful + Giving Thanks but especially asking the Lord for His guidance + will be not & less our own.
   - pray in morning, afternoon, evening

3. Being organize, routinized, in an effort to minimize stress. Use time wisely. (Return to Work)

   — Saturday eve get ready in all that encompasses our ritual & carry that success through into our lives.

   SUN NITE OR MON NITE

Being Joyful

The Power of Forgiveness

"If you hold anything against anyone, forgive him, so that your Father in heaven may forgive you your sins."

—Mark 11:25

All marriage authorities say the same thing: A healthy marriage is one in which forgiveness is practiced. To develop a closer relationship it is vital to give forgiveness but also receive forgiveness with grace. One of the most remarkable stories in the entire Bible is an amazing example of forgiveness, when Jesus forgives a woman caught in the very act of adultery (John 8). It is very good news for all of us imperfect people.

The woman was first brought to Jesus in shame. Jewish law was clear; she could be stoned to death. (We still don't know why the man involved in the sin was missing.) When told of her sin, though, Jesus didn't immediately respond to the woman. He looked into the condescending eyes of the crowd and made this statement: "If any one of you is without sin, let him be the first to throw a stone at her." Jesus then bent down and wrote something in the sand. One by one, people dropped their stones and went back to town, leaving Jesus alone with the woman. Now we hear their intimate conversation. "Woman, where are they? Has no one condemned you?" Sheepishly, probably with tears in her eyes as she sees the people walking away, she replies, "No one, sir." Then Jesus looks into her frightened eyes and says, "Then neither do I condemn you. Go now and leave your life of sin."

Did Jesus say her sin was okay? Not at all. In fact, He told her to leave her life of sin. The words "Neither do I condemn you" are the same ones He says to Christians even now. He loves you completely and unconditionally. And with this amazing love we can find the power to forgive. It's the mother of a young boy innocently shot and killed by a gang member who had the courage to eventually shower forgiveness on the killer and change his life forever. It's the husband who, after hearing of his wife's affair, says, "Honey, that just doesn't sound like you. Let's go to our pastor for counseling and see if we can work this out." It's the daily acts of forgiveness between a husband and wife that may have the most profound impact. Forgiveness is powerful for both the person offering forgiveness and the one receiving it.

The great writer and thinker Philip Yancey says, "Forgiveness halts the cycle of blame and pain, breaking the pain of ungrace." He goes on to say that "forgiveness loosens the stranglehold of guilt in the guilty party, even if a just punishment is still required. Forgiveness creates a remarkable linkage, placing the forgiver on the same side of the party who did the wrong."*

---

*"The Chain of Ungrace," October 9, 2008, *Our Daily Bread.*

FAITH CONVERSATIONS

- What brings you hope from the story of Jesus forgiving the woman caught in adultery? Does anything in the story disturb you?
- When have you experienced forgiveness from me that was especially meaningful to you?
- Is there anything either of us needs to ask forgiveness for? Let's take some time to talk about it.

A STEP CLOSER

THE FORGIVENESS EXERCISE

Confessing our sins to God and asking for His forgiveness and cleansing is incredibly powerful. Take a few moments to privately write separate lists of your sins. Keep your lists between you and God. Now fold up the pieces of paper, put them in a baking pan or some other safe container, and burn them as a symbol of God's forgiveness for your sins. Then read the following verses together and conclude your time with prayer.

THE CONFESSION OF SIN

> "If we confess our sins, he is faithful and just and will forgive us our sins and purify us from all unrighteousness" (1 John 1:9).

> "Have mercy on me, O God, according to your unfailing love; according to your great compassion blot out my transgressions. Wash away all my iniquity and cleanse me from my sin. For I know my transgressions, and my sin is always before me. Against you, you only, have I sinned and done what is evil in your sight, so that you

are proved right when you speak and justified when you judge." (Psalm 51:1–4).

THE ASSURANCE OF FORGIVENESS

"I, even I, am he who blots out your transgressions, for my own sake, and remembers your sins no more" (Isaiah 43:25).

"For as high as the heavens are above the earth, so great is his love for those who fear him; as far as the east is from the west, so far has he removed our transgressions from us" (Psalm 103:11–12).

A Nonnegotiable Date Night

Take delight in honoring each other.

—Romans 12:10 NLT

When the butterflies of early romance flutter away, they are often replaced by the familiar, predictable feelings of long-term attachment. This can be a good thing, but sometimes romance needs to be rekindled. Weekend getaways are wonderful—when you can get away—but day-to-day living quickly eclipses those rare romantic times. We have noticed that friends who keep the spark in their marriages seem to have one thing in common: They have regular, nonnegotiable date nights. Even date nights can become routine, but when a couple proactively injects novelty and energy into their relationship, those exciting butterflies return, re-creating the chemical surges of early courtship.

Do you have a regularly scheduled date with your spouse every week or every other week? If you don't, you may be missing an emotional connection that will keep the fires burning in your relationship. Couples who don't put energy and focus into their dating relationship settle for second best in their marriage bond. It becomes more of a business relationship. I know that I (Jim) have to often ask myself: "Am I giving Cathy only my emotional scraps?" I need—and want—to reserve some of my best energy and focus for our weekly date. For us, this means we try to focus more on each other rather than the latest household bill or our children's schooling.

We have read of a study where researchers instructed married couples to spend ninety minutes a week on a date with each other. The couples who did this tended to enjoy their marriage more than couples who did not take time out for regular dates. The researchers then divided the dating couples into two groups. They challenged one group to do "exciting" activities that appealed to both the husband and wife, like attending a concert or play, and physical activities like hiking or skiing. These are the dates that typically take some time to plan. The other group was asked to do pleasant, more common activities like dining out or going to a movie. Although both groups enjoyed the dates, the couples that shared exciting, more unique activities tended to maintain more romantic intensity.

So make a regular date with your spouse a nonnegotiable appointment. Then plan the date *before* you are heading out of the driveway! At our marriage seminars we invite couples to think outside the box about possible dates. Enjoying a stronger emotional connection will benefit your relationship, and the romance isn't all that bad either!

FAITH CONVERSATIONS

- Are you satisfied with our dating relationship?

- What can we do to enhance the romance in our marriage?
- What have been some of your favorite dates with me over the years?

A STEP CLOSER

Brainstorm twenty dates to help you get started on some creative experiences. (We will give you a few of our favorites that are on the cheap side.)

1. Make a picnic dinner and watch the sunset together from a beautiful spot.
2. Fly a kite and take a walk before a dinner out.
3. Kidnap your spouse right after work for an overnight or a special romantic night. (Make all the arrangements ahead of time for a baby-sitter, money, work, etc.)
4. Have an overnight campout in the backyard.
5. Go out on a date in the morning and be late for work every once in a while.
6.
7.
8.
9.

10.

11.

12.

13.

14.

15.

16.

17.

18.

19.

20.

The Happiness Effect

A cheerful heart is good medicine, but a crushed spirit dries up the bones.

—Proverbs 17:22

Did you know that happiness is contagious? According to a twenty-year study, a person's sense of joy and bright outlook on life can often be determined by how cheerful their friends and especially their spouse are. Actually, this isn't too surprising. The Bible says a great deal about our attitudes, including this insight: "A cheerful look brings joy to the heart, and good news gives health to the bones" (Proverbs 15:30). Laughter just may be the best medicine for a warm, intimate, loving marriage. Studies also show that joy and laughter boost your immunity, improve your mood, ease aches, and relieve stress. Humor actually relieves negative thoughts associated with physical and emotional health problems.

Our good friend Ned Brines quoted his father as saying, "Choose your spouse wisely. This decision will determine 90 percent of your happiness and 100 percent of your unhappiness!" We aren't sure this is universally true, but Ned's parents had a good marriage and the observation definitely makes sense.

There was a season in our life when we realized we had pretty much stopped having fun together. Raising our children, paying the bills, juggling an overcrowded schedule, and other responsibilities had crowded out joy. One small reminder not to take life so seriously was to put a magnet on our refrigerator. It simply read: *"Are we having fun yet?"*

Are you a negative Nancy or a grumpy Greg? If you are, at times your spouse or your kids undoubtedly run from you. We are drained by negativity and by what the Bible calls a "constant dripping," but we are naturally drawn toward laughter, joy, and fun.

Here are two lessons to work on for this "happiness effect": First, *lasting joy is not a matter of what's happening around you, but inside you.* True happiness is tied to internal qualities and character strengths, not external events. This means we have to work on our character and the issues of our heart before we work on the externals. Second, *you can choose to be a person of joy, and it will have a very positive effect on your spouse.* There is an old country song that basically says, "Don't chew me out all day, whine and gripe about me from morning till supper, and then expect me to love you at night." Sure it's a bit harsh, but the point is clear.

Happiness in marriage is a choice, and we have found that if you take care of the special moments, the years will take care of themselves. Here are three building blocks to happiness: (1) Take time to bring pleasure, joy, and good times to you and your spouse. Are you proactive in bringing cheerful energy to your relationship? (2) Engage your life in service and worship. Do you take time to regularly worship God and bring happiness to others through service? (3) Live a purpose-driven life. People whose lives are packed with meaning are almost always happier. Would you say you have a meaningful and purposeful life?

FAITH CONVERSATIONS

- On a scale of 1 to 10 (1 being unhappy and 10 being ecstatic), how do you rate yourself on the "Happiness Scale"? ________
- How would you finish this sentence? "I am most happy and cheerful when ______________________________."
- What could I do or be to make you happier with our marriage?

A STEP CLOSER

THREE BUILDING BLOCKS TO HAPPINESS

Using the three building blocks to happiness (and related questions) below as your guide, write out on the next page activities or steps that you could do together that would bring you more happiness and contentment.

1. Take time to bring pleasure, joy, and good times to you and your spouse. (Are you proactive in bringing cheerful energy to your relationship?)
2. Engage your life in service and worship. (Do you take time to regularly worship God and bring happiness to others through service?)
3. Live a purpose-driven life. (Would you say you have a meaningful and purposeful life?)

SERVANT LOVE OR SELFISH LOVE?

Serve one another in love.

—GALATIANS 5:13

Helen and Lee have one of the finest marriages we know of. They are in their late sixties, and there is still a sparkle in their eyes as they look at each other. They constantly hold hands, and you can tell their love has grown over the years, not diminished like that of so many couples.

One time at a marriage conference, we asked them, "How do you keep your marriage relationship so strong and refreshing?" Helen looked at Lee and Lee smiled. He took her hand and spoke to her, not to us, "Do you remember what I told you the day of our wedding?" She smiled back and said, almost bashfully, "Of course." He said, "I'm going to out-love you every day of our marriage." Helen looked at Lee and said, "And what did I say to you?" She answered her own question, "No, I'm going to out-love you every day." Only then did they focus on us and say, “They’re not fancy words, but we have really tried to live by that promise to each other.”

Marriage is not a 50/50 proposition. It’s about mutual submission and being a servant lover even when we don’t feel like it. In the healthiest of marriages there are seasons when it is more like an 80/20 deal, but that just comes with the territory. Showing honor to each other is about being proactive and intentional with your commitment to serve your spouse. Nobody said it would be easy, but with effort it can be done. Your marriage is worth it. Outdo one another in showing love daily.

Neither of us would at first think we are selfish lovers. We tend to be people pleasers and will try to walk the extra mile even when it isn’t healthy. Yet we have found this concept challenging because we have often placed too many expectations on each other. Your spouse can’t read your mind. The most effective way to share your needs is to spell out those needs to your spouse.

During a tough time at work, our friend Tom asked Kim not to bring up job problems too late at night. It would get his mind spinning and he was having trouble sleeping. Kim needed to bring up the work-related issues for her own peace of mind, but she honored Tom’s request by applying self-discipline to the situation and asking when would be a good time in the next twelve hours to have a talk about work. He was much more ready to tackle her questions over morning coffee. That’s a simple illustration of being a servant lover rather than a selfish lover.

Put all you can into your relationship. You will see results, and even if you don’t right away, you will know you are doing what is right. Relationships that try to “serve one another in love” are the ones that are most long-lasting and fulfilling.

FAITH CONVERSATIONS

- Are there situations right now that make it difficult for you to show me respect? Are there times when it is difficult to love me?
- The Bible says, in Ephesians 5:25–33, "Husbands, *love* your wives . . . and the wife must *respect* her husband" (emphasis added). This Scripture speaks specifically to a wife's need for love and a husband's need for respect.

  Husband: How can I *love* you more effectively?

  Wife: What are specific ways I can show *respect* for you?

A STEP CLOSER

Take time now or in the next few days to talk through these four questions. We have found them to be very helpful in improving our relationship.

- What is right about our marriage?
- What is wrong about our marriage?
- What is confusing about our marriage?
- What is missing from our marriage?

The Purity Code

Guard your heart above all else, for it determines the course of your life.

—Proverbs 4:23 NLT

The road to a safe, intimate marriage relationship always takes the path of purity and fidelity. Sadly, when emotional and sexual infidelity, including pornography, enters a relationship, it breaks apart the relationship almost every time.

The call for sexual purity before marriage is nothing new. But we invite young people—and married couples—to make a lifelong commitment to something we call the *Purity Code.*

In honor of God, my family, and my (future) spouse, I commit my life to sexual purity.

This involves:

- Honoring God with our bodies. (1 Corinthians 6:20)

- Renewing our minds for the good. (Romans 12:2)
- Turning our eyes from worthless things. (Psalm 119:37)
- Guarding our hearts above all else. (Proverbs 4:23)

As we said, as much as unmarried people need to live by the Purity Code, so do married couples. Healthy marriages make sexual integrity a priority. Proactive couples set up wholesome boundaries to guard their hearts from toxic relationships that could damage their marriage. David Carder, in his excellent book *Close Calls,* says he has counseled thousands of people who have experienced adultery. Almost all of them thought they were immune to having an affair.* Because boundaries were not established, these people experienced a growing mutual attraction that could have remained an innocent friendship or shared interest, but because of the lack of healthy boundaries, moved to infatuation, an inordinate clinging to the new partner, and entanglement or sexual involvement.

Today, make a commitment to live by the Purity Code. Do whatever it takes to live above reproach and to "live your life in a manner worthy of the gospel of Christ" (Philippians 1:27). The course of your life will be determined not by how much money you have or the type of house you live in but by the way you have guarded your heart. Enter the right road with purity and integrity. The writer of Proverbs 10:9 said it well: "The man of integrity walks securely." His spouse will walk securely too.

---

*David Carder, *Close Calls: What Adulterers Want You to Know About Protecting Your Marriage* (Chicago: Northfield Publishing, 2008), 9.

FAITH CONVERSATIONS

- How would you finish this sentence? "I commit my purity and integrity to you in these specific ways: _______________."
- Has there been a time when you were concerned about my fidelity?
- How would you finish this sentence? "Of the four steps in the Purity Code, the one I want to commit to working on most is ______________________________."

A STEP CLOSER

Will you commit to a life of sexual integrity? Reread the Purity Code and look up each related Scripture. After a time of praying together, sign your commitment below.

> Do you not know that your body is a temple of the Holy Spirit, who is in you, whom you have received from God? You are not your own; you were bought at a price. Therefore honor God with your body. (1 Corinthians 6:19–20)

THE PURITY CODE PLEDGE

In honor of God, my family, and my spouse, I commit my life to sexual purity. This involves:

- Honoring God with my *body*.
- Renewing my *mind* for the good.
- Turning my *eyes* from worthless things.
- Guarding my *heart* above all else.

Signature:______________________________ Date:__________

Signature:______________________________ Date:__________

The Jesus Creed

"Teacher, which is the greatest commandment in the Law?" Jesus replied, "'Love the Lord your God with all your heart and with all your soul and with all your mind....' And the second is like it: 'Love your neighbor as yourself. All the law and the Prophets hang on these two commandments.'"

—Matthew 22:36–40

Some people have called these words from the mouth of Jesus the super *CliffsNotes* of the Bible. This Jesus Creed is a summary of how to live the Christian life. We are to first love God, and second, love others as you love yourself. Love for God focuses on our spiritual life. Love for others focuses on our relational life, and love for self focuses on our physical and emotional well-being. As a couple, you can do your "life checkups" when you look at this one verse and ask yourselves three questions:

1. Love God (Spiritual Life): Is my heart for God growing or shrinking?
2. Love Others (Relational Life): Am I in a right relationship with my spouse? Others?
3. Love Yourself (Physical/Emotional): Am I physically and emotionally healthy? If not, what is holding me back?

We have found that if we are brutally honest with ourselves, these simple questions will tell us a lot about how we are doing as individuals and as a couple. Many times through our marriage we have had to make U-turns and detours to make the necessary changes to move toward health and healing. People usually don't change unless they are willing to practice the spiritual gift of self-discipline. Paul's advice to his disciple Timothy is sound counsel: "Discipline yourself for the purpose of godliness" (1 Timothy 4:7 NASB). Yes, sometimes it takes raw courage and discipline to make the right decisions about our primary relationships; these would be God, others, and ourselves. With discipline in these areas, more of life seems to make sense and fall into place.

With the thought of discipline in mind, let's look at these three areas of the Jesus Creed.

- *Spiritual:* We find that life lines up better when we worship regularly at church, involve ourselves in a daily time with God as individuals, pray together as a couple, and serve God and others often.
- *Relational:* When our relational priorities are in place—putting God first, our marriage second, children next, vocation, and then other responsibilities—we seem to gain the right focus. But

unfortunately, we too often have a "child-focused" marriage or put our work in front of everything else. Then we wonder why life and relationships aren't working right.

- *Physical/Emotional:* Because of the mess so many marriages and individuals are in, people are now beginning to realize that self-care is necessary too. The discipline of keeping your body in shape by what you eat and how you exercise will enhance every other aspect of your life because it is all tied together. Finding time to rest and then refresh and restore your physical and emotional life is actually a mandate from the Bible. Unfortunately, too many people are living at a pace too fast to take care of their own physical and emotional health.

The Jesus Creed speaks to putting our priorities in the right order. No one said it would be simple, but Jesus has shown us the way.

FAITH CONVERSATIONS

- Of the three issues in the Jesus Creed—Spiritual, Relational, and Physical/Emotional—which area do you/we need to work on most?
- How would you finish this sentence? "The idea of self-discipline comes easy/difficult for me because ______________."
- What can we do as a couple to help each other in these three areas?

A STEP CLOSER

THE ROAD TO GODLINESS

"Discipline yourself for the purpose of godliness" (1 Timothy 4:7 NASB).

With this Scripture in mind, write out two personal and two marriage goals under each of the areas below.

Spiritual:

1. ____
2. ____
3. ____
4. ____

Relational:

1. ____
2. ____
3. ____
4. ____

Physical/Emotional:

1. ____
2. ____
3. ____
4. ____

What Is God Telling You to Do?

On the third day a wedding took place at Cana in Galilee. Jesus' mother was there, and Jesus and his disciples had also been invited to the wedding. When the wine was gone, Jesus' mother said to him, "They have no more wine." "Dear woman, why do you involve me?" Jesus replied, "My time has not yet come." His mother said to the servants, "Do whatever he tells you."

—John 2:1–5

The first miracle we know Jesus performed is one of the Bible's most incredible stories. To set the scene, Jesus and His mother, along with his disciples, are at a wedding in the town of Cana. Wedding celebrations in the time of Jesus were not just for an hour or two, but were at least all-day events, and sometimes went on for several days. The parents would spend their life savings putting on the wedding and feeding all the guests. Of course, it was important to have plenty of food and wine for everyone. It was a known fact that most celebrations would start out with the better wine, and when that was gone, they would serve a cheaper wine.

At this particular wedding, Jesus' mother, Mary, overhears the wine steward say the words the parents never wanted to hear: "We have no more wine." Mary moves over to talk with Jesus to tell Him the problem, and basically Jesus refuses His mother's request by saying, "My time has not yet come" (in other words, no miracles yet). For some reason we imagine Mary having that motherly all-knowing smile (almost a smirk), and then she walks over to the servants and, pointing to her son, says, "Do whatever He tells you." It was probably an awkward moment for all involved, but Jesus relented and whispered to the servants to begin to pour water into the wine barrels. Our guess is that the servants thought Jesus was crazy, but for some unknown reason, they followed His instructions. As the water is poured into the barrels, we read in the Gospels that it immediately became the most wonderful and finest of wines. In fact, the Bible says that the master of the banquet tasted the water turned to wine and praised the bridegroom for saving the best wine for last.

When we read this great story in Scripture, it's easy to miss the most important words: *"Do whatever he tells you."* Five words the servant obeyed that changed the outcome of the wedding. These same words can have a life-changing outcome for our lives as well. Do what He tells you to do. What if you lived your life and your marriage based on those words?

FAITH CONVERSATIONS

- If someone was sent by God to you and said, "Do whatever he tells you," what do you think God would want you to do?

- What is God telling us to do regarding our marriage?
- What do you need from me to help you do what God is calling you to do?

A STEP CLOSER

FIVE ASPECTS OF YOUR LIFE AND YOUR GOALS

Following are five aspects of your life. Write out goals and action steps for the year in each of these areas that you think would be in obedience to God, and then share them with your spouse. (For these and other questions that call for individual responses, you may want to use separate notebooks or pieces of paper.)

1. My relationship with God
2. Our marriage
3. Use of my time
4. Use of my gifts and abilities
5. My health and well-being

The Eternal Perspective

Our light and momentary troubles are achieving for us an eternal glory that far outweighs them all.

—2 Corinthians 4:17

The older we get the more it seems we think about eternity with God. When we were younger, dying seemed a morbid thought. We focused on what we would miss rather than on what we would experience in heaven with God. Now, although we want to live life to the fullest here on earth, we also realize that life on this planet is finite and that one day we will experience something far greater in eternity.

Actually, the eternal perspective has helped our marriage become stronger. In the end, it's mostly relationships that really matter. We seem to fuss and fret over things that will have little bearing on the most important priorities. People who study death and dying say that as a person approaches their last days on earth, their focus becomes much stronger on just two aspects of their life: a right relationship with God, and a right relationship with their loved ones.

Dr. Billy Graham was once invited to a luncheon in his honor in North Carolina. Because of his declining health, he hesitated to go. But his family and friends promised he would not have to give a major address. He could just attend and let them honor him. He finally agreed to go.

After wonderful things were said about him, Billy ended up addressing the gathering, and said, "I'm reminded today of Albert Einstein, the great physicist who was recently honored by *Time* magazine as the Man of the Century. Einstein was once traveling from Princeton on a train when the conductor came down the aisle punching the tickets of each passenger. When he came to Einstein, he couldn't find his ticket. The conductor said, 'Dr. Einstein, I know who you are. We all know who you are. Don't worry about the ticket.' As the conductor continued toward the next car on the train, he turned around and watched Einstein, on his hands and knees, still looking for the ticket. The conductor rushed back and said, 'Dr. Einstein, don't worry. I know who you are. You don't need a ticket. I'm sure you bought one.' Einstein looked at him and said, 'Young man, I, too, know who I am. What I don't know is where I'm going.'"

Having said that, Billy continued, "See this suit I'm wearing? It's a brand-new suit. My family is telling me that I have gotten a little slovenly in my old age. I used to be a bit more fastidious. So I went out and bought a new suit for this luncheon and one more occasion. You know what that occasion is? This is the suit in which I'll be buried. But when you hear I'm dead, I don't want you to immediately remember the suit I'm wearing. I want you to remember this: *I not only know who I am . . . I also know where I'm going.*"

As Christians, we know who we are and where we are going. With this thought in mind about eternity, it draws us back to the "momentary troubles" we have in our marriage, family, and life, and reminds us that those issues don't compare to eternity. Do you have enough of an eternal perspective to focus on the most important relationships instead of becoming bogged down on the lesser? We like how the *New Living Translation* paraphrases Paul's philosophy of life: "For our present troubles are small and won't last very long. Yet they produce for us a glory that vastly outweighs them and will last forever!" Now *that's* the eternal perspective.

FAITH CONVERSATIONS

- How would you finish this sentence? "Here is how the eternal perspective helps my relationship and commitment to you: ____________________________________."
- What problems are you going through that compared to eternity are small but still bug you? Is there anything I can do to give you a better perspective?
- What can we do as a couple to put more of our energy into things that make an eternal difference?

A STEP CLOSER

AT YOUR FUNERAL

With today's message in mind, what do you want to be known for after you die? Take some time to focus on three traits you hope will be brought up at your funeral. Then answer what you can be doing right now to ensure those traits are even stronger in your life.

When you are finished, answer how these traits affect your marriage relationship. Since we are talking about eternity, is there anything else you would like to be said or done at your funeral?

Three Traits

1. ______________________________

2. ______________________________

3. ______________________________

How do these traits affect our marriage?

Other comments about our funerals (sometimes conversations about our death can be difficult, but we know that death is inevitable for all, even in the midst of the eternal promises of God):

____

____

____

____

Longevity in Your Marriage With A.W.E.

Relish life with the spouse you love each and every day of your precarious life. Each day is God's gift. It's all you get in exchange for the hard work of staying alive.

—Ecclesiastes 9:9 The Message

We recently saw a TV news story about the five Estes sisters and their two brothers. Collectively they had been married for 391 years. In an age where nearly half of all new marriages end in divorce, the seven surviving children of C. M. and Minnie Estes have all been wed fifty years or more. The Estes siblings, aged sixty-nine to eighty-four, attribute their marital success in large part to the moral example set by their late parents, who were married fifty-eight years. As we watched the inspiration-filled newscast, we summed up the answers they gave to their secrets to successful marriages with three words: Affection, Warmth, and Encouragement. We call it A.W.E.

Affection: When these couples were interviewed, they all were holding hands. No matter what the age, affection is a very important ingredient in a relationship. Does nagging and negativity ever really work in drawing you closer as a couple? We don't think so either. However, showering your spouse with loving affection does make a difference. A meaningful hug, an extended kiss, flowers, kindness, and those simple words *"I love you"* do bring affection to the forefront of a relationship.

Warmth: One of the constants with these marvelous couples was that it seemed they kept from allowing bitterness, anger, and constant fighting to be a part of their relationships. One of the husbands said, "One of the important things for a successful marriage is having a bad memory." And then they looked at each other and just laughed. In essence, a couple who brings warmth to their relationship has the strength to overlook things that would cause other people to break up. Being intentional about setting an atmosphere of warmth is a discipline. There are times to bring up things that cause tension and times not to do it. In good marriage relationships, couples have a sense of self-control. There is a filter with their words and actions. We loved what another couple shared in that interview: "You've got to let love grow. You both must pitch in, in order for it to work. You have to work at it every day."

Encouragement: The philosopher William James said, "The deepest principle in human nature is the craving to be appreciated." We think most couples would say they feel under-appreciated and under-encouraged. Too many people were raised on shame-based parenting growing up, and when their marriage relationship gets tough, they move back into what their parents tried to do, which is to bring up what's wrong instead of focusing on affirmation. In every relationship there is a time to take withdrawals, but relationships need deposits too. And encouragement is always a deposit. We think many of the marriage issues couples fight over would fade away if they just offered their spouse more encouragement. A daily dose of encouragement does wonders for a difficult relationship.

As we watched the interviews with the Estes family couples, we realized they didn't have anything more in their relationship arsenal than anyone else. Many of these couples did not have easy lives or trouble-free families. What they did possess was a strong commitment to stay together through thick and thin. They saw their marriage as teamwork, and we think they would agree that one of the saving ingredients was that they lived their lives with A.W.E.

FAITH CONVERSATIONS

- As you look at the marriage of a couple you respect, what are some of the ingredients to their success?
- How would you rate our marriage from 1 to 10 on the A.W.E. scale? (1 being "needs immediate help" and 10 being "we've got it down")
- What trait would it take for us as a couple to have the same successful longevity as the Estes family couples?

A STEP CLOSER

A MARRIAGE OF A.W.E.

Take a moment to consider each word represented by A.W.E., and write out what you would like to see from your spouse in each area, and then what you would like to give to your spouse as well.

	What I would like from you	What I would like to give to you
Affection		
Warmth		
Encouragement		

Your Marriage To-Do List

"This is My commandment, that you love one another, just as I have loved you. Greater love has no one than this, that one lay down his life for his friends."

—John 15:12–13 NASB

Do you make to-do lists? We sure do. Both of us are what our kids call list freaks. The only difference is that Cathy makes her multiple lists and follows them, and I make my lists and then lose them! Whether we write them out or not, everyone has to-do lists. We note things as simple as picking up the groceries, calling a friend on her birthday, or paying the taxes on a certain day.

The Bible is much more focused on to-be lists than to-do lists, but throughout the Bible there are a variety of "to-dos" for Christians concerning how we treat each other. They are often referred to as the "one anothers." Here are a few of them that we think directly relate to marriage:

Romans 12:16	Live in harmony with one another.
Romans 15:7	Accept one another.
1 Corinthians 12:25	Care for one another.
Galatians 5:13	Serve one another in love.
Galatians 5:15	Don't spitefully hurt one another.
Galatians 5:26	Don't provoke or envy one another.
Galatians 6:2	Carry one another's burdens.
Ephesians 4:32	Be kind to one another.
Ephesians 4:32	Forgive one another.
Colossians 3:9	Don't lie to one another.
2 Corinthians 1:4	Comfort one another.
Titus 3:3	Don't hate one another.
Hebrews 3:13	Encourage one another.
James 5:9	Don't grumble against one another.
James 5:16	Pray for one another.

These "one anothers" are perfect "to-dos" for a healthy marriage. What if we lived our lives and focused our marriages on these amazing biblical mandates on how to treat our spouse? When the day gets busy and the time runs short, we must admit that we all tend to short-cut this to-do list.

As we look at the life and ministry of Jesus Christ, He obviously lived out the "one anothers." He understood that treating people by the Golden Rule of "doing unto others as you would have them do to you" is not just a philosophy of life, it is *the* way to live life. We love what Mother Teresa once said: "Let no one ever come to you without leaving better and happier." Isn't it interesting to note that the happiest people we know are the ones whose to-do list is filled with loving and serving one another?

FAITH CONVERSATIONS

- What is challenging about the "one another to-do" list for you?
- Which "one another" is hardest for you?
- Today's Scripture says that we are to love one another as Christ loved us. It also says that there is no greater love than when a friend lays down his life for someone else. How can laying down our life be applied to our marriage relationship?

A STEP CLOSER

THE ONE ANOTHER TO-DO LIST

Going back over the list of "one anothers," circle the three that you want to work on this week. Think about how you will specifically accomplish these tasks.

Thank Therapy

Give thanks in all circumstances, for this is God's will for you in Christ Jesus.

—1 Thessalonians 5:18

There have been times when we had to practice "thank therapy" in our relationship to keep our marriage from going toward a not-so-pretty place. We have a high-maintenance marriage—we have to constantly work at keeping our relationship healthy. We have found that even in the midst of tension, if we stop and literally list the things we are thankful for about each other, it reminds us of all the good things in our relationship. Thank therapy is writing down or thinking of at least ten reasons why you are thankful for your spouse.

Let Jim explain. A few years ago, I was speaking at a family conference at the beautiful Mount Hermon Conference Center along the coast in northern California. Over the years, this area of the country, and this conference center, has been one of our favorite stops.

Cathy came up to the conference with me, and we had a wonderful time of ministry to families as well as some downtime on our own for hiking and hanging out at the beach in Santa Cruz. After the conference, we drove to one of our favorite romantic spots on the planet: Carmel, California. We took long walks, ate fun food, and spent extra time just enjoying each other's company.

As we left Carmel, we began to drive down the Pacific Coast on Highway 1. It's an incredibly dramatic drive filled with beauty. As we passed Big Sur, I was basking in the romance of Carmel, when Cathy in a matter-of-fact way leaned over to me and said, "Jim, I think you are getting a double chin." I was looking for something like "Jim, you are my hero" or "Jim, you are an incredible lover," but the double-chin thing for some reason made me really, really mad. (Of course now you are going to turn to the back of the book and look at my chin!) How dare Cathy bring up a flaw that I can be somewhat defensive about while driving along this beautiful highway and right after an amazingly romantic twenty-four hours! She went on gazing at the beauty, and I immediately crawled into my "Jim Cave." Maybe you have your own cave that you crawl into. Frankly, I was mad at her timing.

A few minutes later, as I was sulking and she was gazing, oblivious to her stinging comment, I heard a still, small, nonaudible voice: *"Practice thank therapy."* With gritted teeth I responded (not audibly), *"Thank you, God, for Cathy and her crummy comment."* (Not happy at all about the comment.) Then I softened a bit, looked over at her, and thanked God for a wonderful week with her. I thanked Him for her beauty and fidelity and her deep commitment to Him. I went on thanking Him for the wonderful mother she is to our kids and the many sacrifices she has made over the years. I thanked Him for our friendship and for our romance. I made a mental list of probably thirty reasons why I was thankful for this one who was still gazing out the window and didn't even realize she had wounded me with her silly comment. And then it dawned on me. It really wasn't meant with any harm. Her timing stunk, but hey, with so much to be thankful for about her, did it really matter?

There have been times with tougher issues than the double-chin story that I have had to practice the discipline of thank therapy to make sure I had my priorities straight. What are you thankful for about your spouse? Is it time for you to practice some thank therapy on each other?

FAITH CONVERSATIONS

- How would you finish this sentence? "Here are three things I am thankful for about you."

  (1) ______________________________

  (2) ______________________________

  (3) ______________________________

- How would you finish this sentence? "I am grateful for this special quality of yours: ______________________."
- Why does it sometimes feel like we focus on the negative more than the positive?

A STEP CLOSER

This week keep a journal of at least twenty-five reasons why you are thankful for your spouse, and then give her/him the list. (Jim once wrote a hundred reasons why he was thankful for Cathy, and then cut them up in a hundred pieces and put them in a jar for her to read.)

Three Questions

Test yourselves to make sure you are solid in the faith. Don't drift along taking everything for granted.

—2 Corinthians 13:5 THE MESSAGE

Cathy and I periodically ask ourselves three questions. We want to put them before you today. The way you answer these questions can help you figure out how your relationship with God and your spouse is doing. What's fascinating is if you look at how you are doing emotionally, spiritually, and even physically at any given time, you can usually know the direction your marriage relationship is headed too. Here are the questions:

- Do I like the person I am becoming?
- Is my heart for God shrinking or growing?
- Am I giving my spouse and my children only my emotional scraps?

DO I LIKE THE PERSON I AM BECOMING?

If you like the human being you are becoming, it is often because you are in a good place with God, your spouse, and even yourself. So much of that question has to do with discipline. Paul once wrote to Timothy: "Discipline yourself for the purpose of godliness" (1 Timothy 4:7 NASB). If we are spending regular time reading God's Word and praying, spending healthy doses of time with our spouse, and keeping our body in relatively healthy shape, life seems to go better in our personal life and in our marriage. On the other hand, if we are living an undisciplined life with confused priorities, nothing seems to fit into place.

IS MY HEART FOR GOD SHRINKING OR GROWING?

Far too often when we examine our heart, through either neglect or poor decisions, we find that it isn't in a growing mode. Sometimes it's that we are too busy; other times it's because we aren't disciplined in spending time with God. Some people simply choose poor habits, and that makes their heart for God shrink. For us, it's probably more about living with "attractive distractions." We both tend to bite off more than we can handle, and when the pressures come, we lose the joy of growing in our relationship with God and with each other. We love the way Eugene Peterson paraphrases Romans 9:32 in *The Message* as it describes the people of Israel: "They were so absorbed in their 'God projects' that they didn't notice God right in front of them, like a huge rock in the middle of the road. And so they stumbled into him and went sprawling." Are there attractive distractions in your life that are getting in the way of your heart growing for God?

AM I GIVING MY SPOUSE AND MY CHILDREN ONLY MY EMOTIONAL SCRAPS?

Why is it that we sometimes give our best to others and then don't have anything left to give the ones we love the most? If we are not emotionally present in a relationship, the relationship will grow stale. In a marriage with a lot of tension, there is often at least low-level anger and resentment. When the tension, anger, and resentment aren't harnessed, it often leads to a lack of emotional intimacy. On a diet of little or no emotional intimacy, a marriage can get into trouble very quickly. Being "dangerously tired" will also cause us to give our loved ones only the emotional scraps, and that makes for tired relationships as well.

FAITH CONVERSATIONS

- How would you honestly answer these three questions today?

  Do I like the person I am becoming?
  Is my heart for God shrinking or growing?
  Am I giving my spouse and my children only my emotional scraps?

- What positive steps can we take to resolve the questions that need the most work? What is holding us back?

- Let's rate our emotional intimacy on a scale from 1 to 10 (with 1 being poor and 10 being great). Why is it that?

A STEP CLOSER

Plan a time together this week to work on one of the questions above. What are you going to do and when? Once you have done this, discuss how it went.

Attitude Is Everything

So don't worry about tomorrow, for tomorrow will bring its own worries. Today's trouble is enough for today.

—Matthew 6:34 NLT

We know someone who used to say, "We can't change the cards we're dealt, just how we play the hand." You may not be able to change your circumstance, but your attitude can change, and that makes all the difference in the world. You see, attitude transcends circumstances. When we look at marriages that are working well, we notice that most of the time these people have the same problems as anyone else, but they tend to handle them with a better attitude. Worry, fretting, and negativity fuel an unhealthy relationship. A positive attitude does wonders for any marriage. Wasn't it Martin Luther who said, "You can't keep a bird from flying over your head, but you can keep it from building a nest in your hair"?

One person who exhibited an almost unbelievable attitude was Terry Fox, a young Canadian runner who lost a leg to cancer. Not wanting to give up his beloved running, Terry got a prosthetic leg and continued to run at an amazing level. In fact, he decided to raise money and awareness for cancer research by running from the east coast of Canada to the west coast. But he wasn't content to run just a few miles a day. His goal was to average twenty-six miles a day! That's marathon length. For 143 days straight, he ran close to a marathon each day. There were days right after he ran those twenty-six miles when the TV cameras would zero in on his prosthesis, and you could see his stub red and raw from the pounding it took. When people asked him how he was holding up, he always had the same answer: "I don't know about tomorrow, but I know about today. I'm glad God gave me today. And I'm going to live one day at a time." Talk about inspiring.

Unfortunately, Terry didn't make his cross-country goal. The cancer returned, and after 3,339 miles, he had to stop. The next time the cameras were on Terry, he was in a hospital bed receiving the highest Medal of Honor a Canadian citizen can receive. His face was ashen, his lips purple, and the chemo had taken all his hair. The reporter asked him how he was doing. His reply was a bit weaker but still firm: "I don't know about tomorrow. But I know about today. I'm glad God gave me today. And I am going to live one day at a time." Nine months later he died. Terry Fox lived more in his short twenty-two years than many of us do in a lifetime. One of the many lessons he gave us is that when life gives you lemons, make lemonade, and keep on keeping on.

When talking about relationships, our friend Dr. Henry Cloud says, "I cannot blame them for what I do with what they do to me. I am responsible for how I respond." We have found that so much of a healthy marriage rests on our attitude and not our circumstances.

We have to take responsibility for how we respond to our relationship issues and the circumstances of our life.

FAITH CONVERSATIONS

- What circumstance in our relationship or life is the most difficult to have a positive attitude about? What is holding us back?
- How has fear and worry affected our relationship?
- "I cannot blame them for what I do with what they do to me. I am responsible for how I respond." How does this quote speak to our life?

A STEP CLOSER

Create an Attitude Journal. Make a list of at least five negative things going on in your life and then try to place a better attitude spin on them. Then take time to share these with your spouse.

Negative:	**Positive:**
Example: A child who is making poor choices.	*Example:* We still have a relationship with our son and he shows signs of pulling it together. Scripture says, "Train a child in the way he should go, and when he is old he will not turn from it" (Proverbs 22:6). This is a great promise to hold on to.

Negative:	**Positive:**

No Regrets

I have fought the good fight, I have finished the race, and I have remained faithful.

—2 Timothy 4:7 NLT

Thomas Carlyle, a great British writer in the nineteenth century, was already well established in his career when he married another writer, Jane Welsh. Obsessed with his writing, though, he took little time to nurture their relationship. Even when Jane became very ill, Carlyle wasn't there for his wife.

After Jane died, Carlyle sat in her bedroom, regretting how little time he had spent with her because of all the other "important" things he was doing. It was then that he noticed her diary sitting on the bedside stand. One page simply read: *"Yesterday he spent an hour with me and it was like heaven. I love him so."* He turned another page. *"I listened all day to hear his footsteps in the hall, but now it is too late and I guess he won't come today."*

Carlyle continued to read until he was overcome with emotion. He threw the diary down and ran out of his house. His friends found the grieving man at Jane's graveside with his face buried in the ground and tears rolling down his cheeks. He just kept saying over and over, "If only I had known, if only I had known, but it's too late now." Fifteen years later he died with a mountain of regret.

Sometimes we allow confused priorities to get in the way of the most important relationships. It's important for a marriage to get off to a good start, but we want our marriage to finish well too. We're sure you want this too. Make your marriage the priority it is meant to be.

FAITH CONVERSATIONS

- What part of this story can you relate to?
- What could you or I do to live with fewer regrets in our relationship?
- At the end of your life, what would you like to be said about you?

A STEP CLOSER

Look at the Scripture of the day and write out a paragraph of what you would hope could be said about your marriage at the end of your life.

Dad

"Seek first his kingdom and his righteousness, and all these things will be given to you as well."

—Matthew 6:33

Jim's father recently died. He was eighty-nine and had lived a good life. When I (Jim) was growing up, Dad had his issues. He was a functioning alcoholic, but in his sixties he gave up drinking and never looked back. In his eighties, he was quite frail, broke his hip, and then after a hip replacement he contracted pneumonia and never made it out of the hospital.

A week before he died, I was sitting in the convalescent hospital with my dad. A new physical therapist came to visit and must have gotten the charts confused. Enthusiastically she said, "Hi, Bob! Are you ready for physical therapy?" I just smiled, knowing he was instead ready for hospice care. I decided not to say anything and watch what would happen. She helped him up, and she could see he was very weak. "Bob, how did you break your hip?" My dad looked her right in the eye and said, "It was a motorcycle accident." This frail eighty-nine-year-old was so convincing that the therapist looked at me. I just shrugged my shoulders and smiled. Dad went right on telling her that he had always wanted to ride my brother's motorcycle, and so one day when my brother wasn't home, he got on the bike and rode it around the neighborhood. The problem was he didn't know how to stop the motorcycle, and when he drove it up onto our backyard patio, he put it right through the patio door. The physical therapist gave me another look. I whispered, "That did occur—about forty-seven years ago!" My memory involves coming home from elementary school to find my brother's motorcycle in our living room with gas, oil, glass, and blood on the carpet with the bike.

The physical therapist smiled. Dad was so positive and so grateful. She then asked, "Do you have other children, Bob?" He said, "Yes, I have four boys, and I'm proud of all four of them." This took me a bit by surprise, and tears welled up in my eyes to hear my dad say to a stranger that he was proud of me. Then I looked at the woman, and there were tears in her eyes as well. He went on to say, "I've lived a good life. I am deeply grateful to God and my family. I was married to his mom (he pointed to me) for fifty-three years. She is in heaven waiting for me, and I'm ready to be there." More tears. Then he added, "After his mom died, I married one of her best friends, Virginia. She has been like an angel to me. I am a very fortunate man." By this time the woman was crying, I was crying, and she had brought him back to his bed. We met outside. With tears still in her eyes, she said, "Your father has a beautiful attitude. He is the reason I do what I do. He is so inspiring, even at the end of his life."

I sat outside the room for just a bit and thought, *How like God!* Dad was saying that he was proud of my brothers and me. Believe me, we have made our share of mistakes, but he was still proud of his kids, just like God is proud of you, His child. Dad also taught me to have more of an eternal perspective that kept bringing me back to having a grateful heart. He was thankful to God and thankful for the ones he loved. Later, when I arrived home and told Cathy my story, I just held her and told her I wanted to be more like my dad. As I mentioned earlier, authorities on death and dying tell us that when someone is about to die they seek a right relationship with God and a right relationship with their loved ones. At the end of life, they finally get their priorities straight. I hope it doesn't take me that long.

FAITH CONVERSATIONS

- What are your top priorities at this point in life?
- Are there relationships you would like to improve upon?
- A right relationship with God and our loved ones: What can we begin doing today to move in that direction?

A STEP CLOSER

Together, come up with someone you both know who inspires you to get your priorities in order. What are the qualities they possess that you would like to have? What can you do this week as a couple to work on this?

Accountability Makes a Marriage Stronger

Confess your sins to each other and pray for each other so that you may be healed. The earnest prayer of a righteous person has great power and produces wonderful results.

—James 5:16 NLT

Five men meet in a living room with coffee in one hand and a Bible in the other. They talk about the local sports team, they complain about politics and the economy. Then they pull out their Bibles and begin to study a passage or theme. The study moves quickly to personal life, and at the end of the meeting they share prayer requests and their focus for the week. At lunch two women meet for their regular time of sharing and prayer. One of the women is a bit older, and although she sees herself as more of an equal, the younger woman calls her a mentor. In these times of accountability and support, marriages are healed and children are helped. Faith is dissected and grown. Prayers are offered and answered.

Accountability is at the foundation of experiencing a marriage and family of integrity. The strength of personal accountability in your own life will strengthen the integrity of your marriage and your kids. We believe that we are better spouses and parents because we have worked hard at developing accountability relationships in our life. If you need a place to start, let us offer a few tips.

Seek out other like-minded people who are interested in developing an accountability relationship. As a rule, same-sex relationships work best in accountability settings. Potential participants may include someone you admire and desire as a mentor, peers, or someone you might want to mentor. Finding the right people to be in a supportive relationship sometimes takes work and almost always takes time to develop an honest, authentic relationship. Make sure the people you enter into an accountability relationship with are trustworthy. Grant them (or the person) access into your life for the purpose of holding you accountable. This means you have to be willing to be vulnerable and honest, and we believe you have to meet somewhat regularly for the process to work. We have had individual accountability partners and participated in support groups. Both ways work. Women tend to find accountability easier than men (at least that has been our experience).

Ask and answer the sometimes difficult questions. Honesty is an absolute must to experience true growth. Jim is in a group where he meets with five of his mentors every Tuesday morning. He also meets with one of his best friends, Dr. Jon Wallace, the president of Azusa Pacific University. Jim and Jon tend to ask the tough questions of each other. Jon actually puts these questions and answers before his board at the university once a year.

1. Do you practice confession of sin? What is the evidence?
2. What acts of personal spiritual renewal are you practicing, such as Bible study, prayer, reflection, and solitude?
3. What is the evidence that you are maintaining your family as a priority in your life?
4. What are evidences of personal, spiritual, and professional growth in your life?
5. Are you maintaining life-giving relationships? What is the evidence?
6. What is the evidence that you are living a balanced life?

Developing accountability is not a program but a mindset. The issue isn't answering particular questions but finding a person or persons who know your heart. We were not meant to handle brokenness or heartbreak alone. We were not meant to raise our kids alone. We definitely weren't meant to draw closer together as a couple without the help of others to whom we are accountable.

Do you have this kind of relationship? If not, what is holding you back? You will develop a much more vibrant marriage relationship if you have other people in your life who keep you honest, ask the right questions, and show you the same grace and mercy that God shows you.

FAITH CONVERSATIONS

- On a scale of 1 to 5 (1 being minimal and 5 being sufficient), rate the accountability you have in your life.

- Is there a person or group with whom you would you like to take a step closer in accountability? _______________________.
- What could we do to have more accountability in our relationship?

A STEP CLOSER

DEVELOPING MORE ACCOUNTABILITY

Write out five questions that you would like to have your spouse ask you on a regular basis. These questions should be supportive and helpful, not nagging. You can make up the questions or take them from the list below. (These pretty much get right to the point.)

- Have you been with a person of the opposite sex anywhere during the past week that might have been seen as compromising?
- Have any of your financial dealings lacked integrity this week?
- Have you exposed yourself to any sexually explicit material this week?
- Have you spent adequate time in Bible study and prayer this week?
- Have you given priority to your family?
- Have you fulfilled the mandate of your calling?
- Have you lied to me?

Keep On Treasuring

Each one of you also must love his wife as he loves himself, and the wife must respect her husband.

—Ephesians 5:33

One cold winter day in a Washington, DC, metro station, a musician set up his spot and began to play a violin. His violin case was open to receive donations from any who would pass by and drop a coin into his rather ragged container. Most of the people on that busy day briskly walked past him as he played six pieces from Bach for about forty-five minutes. Later someone calculated that at least a thousand people had walked past him. Most didn't seem to notice him at all; a few smiled and dropped some coins in his case. Only a child begged his mother to stop and "listen to the pretty music." During this "concert in the metro," the musician wearing tattered clothes received offerings from twenty-seven people, totaling just shy of thirty-two dollars. Hardly anyone stopped to fully appreciate the music.

All those people didn't realize the violinist was Joshua Bell, one of the greatest musicians in the world. And just that week he had played before a sold-out theater where the seats averaged more than one hundred dollars a ticket. The violin he played was a Stradivarius worth $3.5 million.

When we heard this story, we wondered where the places are in our lives that we take beauty for granted or miss opportunities to treasure the gift of marriage and family we have been given by God. Far too often we walk right past opportunities to appreciate each other for the simple things.

Do you ever take your spouse for granted? If you are like us, you do. How about making a pact together to love each other equally when things go right in your life and when things go wrong? If you get a second chance, grab it. Value your marriage for what it is: a precious gift from God.

Someone once told us to "forgive quickly, kiss slowly, and enjoy the little things, because one day you may look back and realize they were the big things." God never promised marriage would be without problems. He just promised it would be worth it. Scripture says, "Love your wives." The actual Greek meaning is "keep on loving," or even *"keep on treasuring"* your wives. This command, of course, goes for wives toward their husbands as well. The goal is oneness. "For this reason a man will leave his father and mother and be united to his wife, and they will become one flesh" (Genesis 2:24).

FAITH CONVERSATIONS

- What areas of our relationship do we sometimes take for granted?
- Let's take a moment to affirm in each other traits that we haven't affirmed for a long time.
- When we look at our marriage as a gift from God, how does it change the way we think about our relationship?

A STEP CLOSER

YOUR MARRIAGE INVENTORY

Take a few moments to write down ten things that are right about your marriage and share the list with your spouse.

1.
2.
3.
4.
5.
6.
7.
8.
9.
10.

Jumping to Conclusions

Finally, all of you should be of one mind. Sympathize with each other. . . . Be tenderhearted, and keep a humble attitude. Don't repay evil for evil. Don't retaliate with insults when people insult you. Instead, pay them back with a blessing. That is what God has called you to do, and he will bless you for it.

—1 Peter 3:8–9 NLT

What is it that causes couples to jump to wrong conclusions? Sometimes we are too quick to blame our spouse when we don't have all the information. Or we misunderstand what is trying to be communicated and react badly. Cathy and I know all about this. We are experts at jumping to the wrong conclusion. Here is a common Jim-phrase: "In my humble opinion . . ." Here is a common Cathy-phrase (often with a smirk on her face): "In his humble opinion, he thinks he's always right . . ." Today's Scripture reading from First

Peter shows us how to treat one another and why it's not good to jump to conclusions.

Some time ago, our pastor told a story in church that was based on a poem by Valerie Cox. It all started when a woman bought a bag of cookies and sat down with a book to wait to board her flight. Not much later, she noticed an older gentleman sitting next to her grab a cookie from the bag between them. Not wanting to make a scene, she shifted the bag closer to her. A few moments went by, and she heard some rustling, and sure enough he'd taken another cookie, smiled, and put it in his mouth. For every cookie she ate, he grabbed another, until the very last cookie, which he broke, offering half to her. The woman was furious. *Who did he think he was?* She gathered her things and boarded the plane. Once in her seat, she opened her purse and found . . . her unopened bag of cookies.

Has something like this ever happened to you? Have you ever made a wrong assumption? Of course you have. Haven't we all? And frankly, on most occasions we would do better to be slow to judge. The emphasis is on the word *slow.* The Bible says, "Everyone should be quick to listen, slow to speak and slow to become angry" (James 1:19). Just think how much better our relationships would be if we put this verse into practice. And then there are the wise words of Jesus: "Do not judge, or you too will be judged" (Matthew 7:1), and "First get rid of the log in your own eye; then you will see well enough to deal with the speck in your friend's [spouse's] eye" (Luke 6:42 NLT). And hey, even if your first impression was correct and you ended up losing half a bag of cookies, remember, it really isn't all that important anyway.

FAITH CONVERSATIONS

- Can you remember a time when you jumped to a wrong conclusion about me? How did you handle the situation? How would you handle it today?
- What can we do to be less judgmental of each other?
- After rereading today's Scripture (1 Peter 3:8–9), what are some ways we can be a blessing to each other?

A STEP CLOSER

A WORD OF APOLOGY AND A WORD OF BLESSING

Make or buy a card for each other this week and write out an apology for a time when you jumped to a wrong conclusion. Then add a note filled with blessing and love. Read the cards to each other.

A Love Story

Love is patient and kind. Love is not jealous or boastful or proud or rude. It does not demand its own way. It is not irritable, and it keeps no record of being wronged. It does not rejoice about injustice but rejoices whenever the truth wins out. Love never gives up, never loses faith, is always hopeful, and endures through every circumstance.

—1 Corinthians 13:4–7 NLT

Our friends Scott and Jean told us an amazing love story. The hero and heroine are Scott's parents, who have been married for over fifty years. Like everyone, they had their ups and downs in their marriage and family. And in recent years, life got really tough when Scott's mom had to move into a nursing home because she had Alzheimer's disease. Scott said he and Jean wanted his dad to live closer to them, but he wasn't willing to move away from Scott's mom.

"Does she recognize him?" we asked.

"No, but that doesn't matter to Dad," replied Scott, adding that she hadn't recognized his dad for over four years.

"Does he visit her often?"

"Every single day. In fact, he has breakfast with her and feeds her from his own plate. He then cleans her up and gets her ready for her day."

Even Scott would occasionally press his dad about why he kept up the daily visits. "He always answers with the same words: *'She doesn't know me, but I still know who she is.'* "

Scott continued his parents' love story. "She likes it when Dad sings to her. She especially likes to hear 'Jesus loves me, this I know, for the Bible tells me so. . . .' So every day before he leaves her, he sings that simple song and places the sign of the cross on her forehead."

A love so pure, a love so complete.

At your wedding, you might have committed to vows similar to these: "I, ______________, take you, ______________________, to be my husband/wife. I promise and covenant before God and these witnesses to be your loving and faithful wife/husband—in plenty and in want, in sickness and in health, in joy and in sorrow, in good times and hard times, with God's grace and strength, as long as we both shall live."

Scott's dad recited those sacred vows over fifty years ago. And those vows are now on our bathroom mirror to remind us of that beautiful day when we committed our lives to each other. Your life, like ours, is probably a bit more complicated than when you were newlyweds. You might carry more worries of the world. But it's good to remember the day you committed to love each other until "death do us part."

We have never met Scott's dad, but we are grateful to him for showing us lasting love. And we are committed to living out those vows like they were new and fresh. How about you?

FAITH CONVERSATIONS

- Why do you think it is difficult, at times, to keep our vows?
- How would you finish this sentence? "I could better keep my vows to you by ______________________."
- How would you finish this sentence? "If I could ask just one thing from you, it would be ______________________."

A STEP CLOSER

THE BIBLE'S LOVE CHAPTER

First Corinthians 13 is often called the Love Chapter. Verses 4 to 7 are particularly inspiring:

> "Love is patient and kind. Love is not jealous or boastful or proud or rude. It does not demand its own way. It is not irritable, and it keeps no record of being wronged. It does not rejoice about injustice but rejoices whenever the truth wins out. Love never gives up, never loses faith, is always hopeful, and endures through every circumstance" (NLT).

Circle the words or phrases that each of you wants to work on this week. What is one action step that you will take to move from mere words to actions?

H.A.L.T.

The Lord is my shepherd, I shall not want. He makes me lie down in green pastures; He leads me beside quiet waters. He restores my soul; He guides me in the paths of righteousness for His name's sake.

—Psalm 23:1–3 NASB

It is amazing how four simple letters—H-A-L-T—can keep so many people from making poor decisions. We believe they can also transform a stagnant marriage into a vibrant one.

In the alcohol-and-drug-recovery world, the acronym H.A.L.T. helps keep addicts from relapsing by reminding them not to get too Hungry, Angry, Lonely, or Tired. These same words are important in keeping a marriage together.

HUNGRY

Dr. David Carder, who wrote a great book on avoiding affairs, says, "Food and sex are basic needs. Alcoholics always drink when they are hungry. This is the feeling of emptiness that causes some to eat emotionally, others to drink, still others to act out sexually."* One of the most incredible teachings of the apostle Paul is "Your body is a temple of the Holy Spirit. . . . Therefore honor God with your body" (1 Corinthians 6:19–20). It would take a lot more space than this to unpack all the meaning in this truth. But authorities tell us that our body is closely linked with our spirit and actions. Having a healthy body is often one of the first steps toward building healthy relationships. If you are eating comfort foods because of your stress, you can be pretty sure that neither your body nor your spouse is getting your best. There are times when Jim comes home from work famished because he forgot to eat. When he is hungry, he definitely isn't as sensitive to my needs.

ANGRY

Anger is a common thread throughout many—dare we say most—marriages. After all, you can pretty much find a reason to be angry with your spouse (and teenagers!) 24/7/365. If anger is not dealt with between a couple, bitterness and resentment begin to take over the relationship, and this blocks growth and intimacy. The Bible says clearly, "Do not let the sun go down while you are still angry" (Ephesians 4:26). This doesn't mean you won't *get* angry, it just means you will have to deal with the anger and not allow it to fester. Continual anger toward your spouse will involve a lack of forgiveness, and this blocks closeness. Little annoyances tend to become larger-than-life issues when anger isn't dealt with quickly.

LONELY

There is an epidemic of lonely couples in the world today. The pace of life, Internet use, children's schedules, TV, and a host of

*Carder, *Close Calls: What Adulterers Want You to Know About Protecting Your Marriage,* 163.

other (even positive) priorities get in the way of couples connecting. Loneliness, when unguarded, can become anything from an illicit affair to a general lack of togetherness. We know one couple who recently got a divorce not because of infidelity, but because they simply woke up one day and said, "There is nothing left of our relationship. We ignored our loneliness and pain for so long we just drifted out of love." The answer to overcoming loneliness is to be proactive about connecting with your spouse. It's a matter of establishing a priority and then making it happen. Here's a good phrase to remember: "Don't try to prioritize your schedule; schedule your priorities." Is your spouse a priority on your weekly schedule? What would he or she say?

TIRED

Too many couples want to connect and be closer, but frankly, they are just too tired to care. Exhaustion is one of the major causes of brokenness in relationships. What's the answer? You may not like this, but the only answer we can find is to rest. Our bodies were not meant to go at the pace most of us go. Eventually, the body breaks down, but often the breakdowns happen first in our relationship with our spouse. Exhaustion does damage and rest heals. We aren't suggesting everyone move to a commune somewhere in the countryside. It's more complicated than that. We have to take charge of our life where we live in the midst of a pace of life that kills relationships. During the creation process, even God rested on the seventh day, and the Bible says He was refreshed. If your pace of life is out of control and you find yourself exhausted most of the time, you are probably not living in the will of God. Can we say it any more bluntly?

So the answer is to H.A.L.T. and make better decisions about each area of life. Do it for your health and the health of your marriage. It will restore your soul and put you on the right path.

FAITH CONVERSATIONS

- Of these four moods—Hungry, Angry, Lonely, and Tired—which one do you struggle with the most?
- Did the Lord prompt any ideas as we read this message today? Are there any practical life changes that we should try?
- The Scripture today says that God restores our souls. What is our part in the restoration process?

A STEP CLOSER

H.A.L.T.

Take each word in the acronym H.A.L.T. and write out the needs in your life and how they affect your marriage. Share with each other what you come up with, and then talk about practical answers to your insights.

Need	Effect on Our Marriage Relationship
Hungry	
Angry	
Lonely	
Tired	

Your Body and Your Marriage

Do you not know that your body is the temple of the Holy Spirit, who is in you, whom you have received from God? You are not your own, you were bought at a price. Therefore honor God with your body.

—1 Corinthians 6:19–20

The Hebrew people of the Bible had a much higher and more complicated view of the human body than most of us do. To the Hebrews, a person's body was intricately connected to her mind and heart. The body was considered sacred. Even in the Scripture verses for today, the apostle Paul calls our body the "temple of the Holy Spirit."

By the looks of mainstream America, we haven't done a very good job of taking care of our temple of God. Not everyone can have the body of an Olympic champion, but we do think that if a person doesn't take care of his body, he probably isn't taking care of other issues in his life either. Even in churches today we hear preachers talking about certain sins, but few talk about gluttony or other matters of the body. We realize it's a complicated subject, and for many people, there are not simple answers. However, healthy people tend to take care of their body. We buy into a three-pronged approach to taking care of our bodies: diet, sleep, and exercise.

Diet. Daniel, of Bible fame, showed us over four thousand years ago that eating right would give you a health advantage. Studies now show that healthy, nutritious eating will make you feel better. When you feel better you will have more energy to put into your relationships. Guilty pleasures are fine in moderation. Our splurges most often have the word *chocolate* in them! But a balanced and health-conscious diet is more than just a good idea from a nutritionist; it is good for your marriage as well.

Sleep. In Bible days, people most likely got enough sleep because they didn't have the complications of electricity, television, computers, phones, and so on. They went to bed when the sun went down and they woke up when it rose. Today health and many relationships suffer because of lack of sleep. Sleep heals, sleep soothes, and sleep gives you perspective. Sleep reduces stress, improves a poor disposition, and even helps your memory. Here is one of our communication principles: "If you are in conflict with your spouse and both of you are too tired to talk it through, make an appointment for the next day and get some sleep." We find that a good night's sleep does wonders for healthy relationships.

Exercise. We are big on exercise. Er . . . actually, Cathy is much more disciplined than I am, but the benefits of exercise are numerous and we believe relate directly to marriage health as well. According to the Mayo Clinic, exercise:

- Improves your mood
- Combats chronic disease

- Helps you manage weight
- Strengthens your heart and lungs
- Produces better sleep
- Puts the spark back in your sex life
- Can be—gasp—fun!

Our bodies are connected to every aspect of our lives. Don't abuse the gift God has given you. Treat your body as the temple of God that it is.

FAITH CONVERSATIONS

- When reading 1 Corinthians 6:19–20, what do you think about your body being the temple of God and that we are to honor God with our body?
- Which area do you need to work on most? Diet, sleep, or exercise?
- How do these areas affect our marriage?

A STEP CLOSER

DIET—SLEEP—EXERCISE

With the old adage in mind, "If you fail to plan, you plan to fail," put together a simple plan to help each of you honor God with your body. Write out simple goals related to diet, sleep, and exercise, and then discuss how you can encourage each other to work toward these goals.

Goals	Encouragement
Diet	
Sleep	
Exercise	

When I Relax, I Feel Guilty

They were so absorbed in their "God projects" that they didn't notice God right in front of them, like a huge rock in the middle of the road. And so they stumbled into him and went sprawling.

—Romans 9:32 The Message

One underlying problem of people who lack marital intimacy is stress. Everyone has some stress in their life, but far too many couples are out-of-control busy and tell us that their lives are just too hectic. Stress just may be the number-one intimacy breaker for couples.

Our advice is to ruthlessly seek to eliminate stress from your life. At the risk of sounding overly simplistic, you may need to practice what the Hebrews called the *Sabbath*. The word literally means "to rest." Do you have regular times of rest? If you don't, then you are in or rapidly moving toward burnout. Even God rested on the seventh day of Creation. The Bible says, "He rested and was refreshed." In

Hebrew, the word for *refreshed* was more like "he rested and exhaled." We love that word picture. Sometimes we just need to relax and exhale. Couples who are wound up too tight don't draw close to each other. There is an old Greek adage that says, "You will break the bow if you keep it always bent." How tight is your bow?

Everybody has to figure out what restores them best, but here are a few ideas:

- Take some time off. Go on a do-nothing vacation.
- Spend time with friends who replenish you as individuals and as a couple.
- Don't stay up late. A good night's sleep reduces tension and pressure.
- Pray and meditate on God's Word.
- Ditch a responsibility (that won't leave anyone in the lurch) and take a picnic lunch to the park.
- Read a book.
- Bring him/her breakfast in bed.
- Have a hot bubble bath ready for her after a long day.
- Go fishing.
- Fly a kite.
- Do whatever it takes to relax, and then make it a regular part of your life.

Simple ideas? Maybe. The sad thing is that most people are too stressed out to try to do anything about it.

FAITH CONVERSATIONS

- How is your stress-o-meter? On a scale from 1 to 10 (1 being extremely stressed and 10 being relaxed), how would you rank yourself today?
- The Scripture for today, which is taken from *The Message*, describes people who were so busy and distracted that they couldn't see God right in front of them. Does that ever happen to you?
- How would you finish this sentence? "You could help me reduce the stress I feel by ________________________."

A STEP CLOSER

MAKE EVERY DAY A LESS STRESSFUL DAY

Does anything seem to create stress for you on a daily basis? Brainstorm at least ten practical de-stressors for you individually and as a couple. Write them down and then talk about how and when you could try them.

DE-STRESSORS

1.

2.

3.

4.

5.

6.

7.

8.

9.

10.

God Meets Our Deepest Needs

[God] said, "My grace is all you need. My power works best in weakness." So now I am glad to boast about my weaknesses, so that the power of Christ can work through me. That's why I take pleasure in my weaknesses, and in the insults, hardships, persecutions, and troubles that I suffer for Christ. For when I am weak, then I am strong.

—2 Corinthians 12:9–10 NLT

During the writing of this book, several issues in our life have made us turn to today's Scripture often—especially "My grace is all you need. My power works best in weakness." Jim was diagnosed with prostate cancer. We are strongly aware that there are much worse cancers to have, but it still causes us to rethink life. Plus, he is the guy who wasn't sick with even a cold for six years in a row. About the same time a close family member moved in with us to escape an abusive marriage situation. Then, with the spiraling economy,

HomeWord has fallen on some tough financial times and we have had to cut back.

Others experience much worse situations than this, but crisis is always self-defined, so this year has been our crisis year. Just the other day we reread the words from the pen of Paul, "When I am weak, then I am strong." As we prayed together, we felt God's message to us was "I am the All-Sufficient One" or *El Shaddai,* from the Hebrew language. God never promised to take away our problems, but He did promise to meet our deepest needs, often through our weakness.

We don't know your situation. You may be feeling inadequate and somewhat helpless, as we have many times this year. In tough times, call out to God—the All-Sufficient One. Give Him your circumstances, fear, worry, and sorrow. Thank Him for walking every step of the way with you. Our experience is that we can rest assured that God meets our deepest needs. In our weakness, we find His strength.

The great promise in Psalm 23 is "Even though I walk through the valley of the shadow of death, I will fear no evil, for you are with me" (Psalm 23:4). God doesn't promise to take away our pain and sorrows or even our problems. He does promise to walk with us through it all and comfort us. In your weakness, turn to God for strength.

FAITH CONVERSATIONS

- What do you think Paul means when he says, "When I am weak, then I am strong"? How does this phrase apply to our life and to our marriage?
- When have you seen God meet your deepest need?

- How would you finish this sentence? "If there is one thing I need from God right now it is ______________________________."

A STEP CLOSER

TURNING YOUR WEAKNESS INTO STRENGTH

Make a list together of five weaknesses in your marriage. Admit them to God and talk about how they could become strengths. Choose one weakness each of you will work on this week.

Think Generationally

For I will pour water on the thirsty land, and streams on the dry ground; I will pour out my Spirit on your offspring, and my blessing on your descendants.

—Isaiah 44:3

You may be like us. We call ourselves the "transitional generation" in our extended family. The Bible is clear that we inherit the sins of a previous generation; in fact, the same sin-weaknesses and sin-tendencies sometimes stretch over three or four generations. Cathy and I grew up in somewhat dysfunctional families. There was alcoholism, adultery, and emotional instability within our family systems. Since our families didn't have a strong Christian background, our conversions to Christianity as teenagers reset the course of our lives. One week after Cathy graduated from college, we got married. We had been leaders at our university and then called to Christian ministry, so we thought marriage would be easy. It wasn't.

We soon realized that to make our marriage healthier than previous generations, we would have to overcome negative family patterns. We could either repeat the sins of the past or recover. We chose to recover, but didn't fully realize the cost of breaking the chains of dysfunction. It is hard work, especially when you bring children into the mix and add the stress of life, work, and relationships. However, it is worth it.

No matter what your family background is, think generationally. You can make your life and marriage fuller and better than that of your parents, grandparents, and great-grandparents. As the transitional generation, you not only change your own life, but you change it for your children and their children.

Burt and Rhonda Wilson were high school sweethearts. They both became Christians through a Young Life ministry at their local high school. In all, their parents had been married seven different times—not exactly good role models for marriage. Burt and Rhonda wanted to break family patterns and commit to living generationally. It wasn't always easy, they say, but they did the work needed to make their marriage and family life succeed. Today they can count more than fifty-five children, grandchildren, and great-grandchildren that are following Christ. Of that group there are pastors, teachers, missionaries, and doctors, all using their gifts to create change in the world. And there has been only one divorce in the last three generations. It is pretty incredible to see what one couple that is committed to being a part of the transitional generation can pull off with God's guidance.

How about you? Are you in position to be the transitional generation of your family? Today will you reaffirm this verse: "Choose today whom you will serve. . . . But as for me and my family, we will serve the Lord" (Joshua 24:15 NLT)?

FAITH CONVERSATIONS

- What issues did you most likely inherit from your family? Which is the most difficult issue to overcome?
- How can I help you?
- Read Psalm 78:6 and Psalm 145:4. How do these words give us hope?

A STEP CLOSER

BECOMING A TRANSITIONAL GENERATION PEOPLE

Here are four action steps for becoming a transitional generation person. Below the action step, write out a goal for working on one area of your life from each of these points. Share these goals with each other. Talk about how you can support one another in this journey.

1. You must have a desire to recover and not repeat the sins of the past. ____

2. You must be willing to repair your own brokenness.

   ____

3. You must be willing to seek the counsel of others.

   ____

4. You must be open to obeying God's Word as it applies to your marriage and your family. ______________________________

   ____

Reactions Speak Louder Than Words

"And why worry about the speck in your friend's eye when you have a log in your own? How can you think of saying to your friend, 'Let me get rid of the speck in your eye,' when you can't see past the log in your own eye? Hypocrite! First get rid of the log in your own eye; then you will see well enough to deal with the speck in your friend's eye."

—Matthew 7:3–5 NLT

Becky decided to leave her husband. She had had enough. She packed her bags along with her fourteen-month-old son and left home. With tears in her eyes, she walked into her mother's house and announced her decision.

Her mother hugged her and said, "Before you leave Bill, I have one more task for you to complete." Her mom then took out a pen and paper. She drew a vertical line down the middle of the paper. She told Becky to make a list of all the things that made Bill impossible to live with. That was easy for Becky to do. The list filled the page. She listed his bad habits and what he didn't do for her, like bring her nice presents or help much with the housework.

Becky assumed her mom would then ask her to write down his good traits on the other side of the paper. Her mom told Becky that she already knew his good qualities. Instead, she wanted her daughter to write out next to every bad trait, how she responded to each. "What do you do when he does something you don't like?" "What is your reaction?"

This took Becky by surprise, but she began to write, noting things like "I pout and cry and get angry" and "I give him the silent treatment." When Becky finished the page, her mother took the paper and cut it in half. She handed only the column of Becky's responses back to her. She suggested that Becky go home and think about things. Her mom would watch the baby. "Pray about them, Becky. If you still want to leave Bill, Dad and I will do all we can to help you."

Becky drove back to her house. That day she focused on how she responded to Bill, how petty and negative her reactions could be. She spent the next several hours asking God for forgiveness. She asked for strength, guidance, and wisdom. She realized that she was honestly blessed with a good man—not a perfect man, but a good one. She remembered her vow to Bill five years earlier in the presence of family, friends, and God to love and honor him in good times and bad times. She jumped back in her car and drove to her parents' house. She picked up her baby and drove back home in time to meet her husband after work.

Becky knew the difference in their marriage would come from within. From that day forward she would try to be mindful not only of her *actions* but her *reactions* as well.

FAITH CONVERSATIONS

- How would you finish this sentence? "After reading this story, I believe my reactions are often ______________________." (Fill in a word that best describes how you react.)
- What keeps us from having better reactions when we have trouble?
- What do you think I can do to be a more effective *reactor* to our issues?

A STEP CLOSER

PROBLEMS AND REACTIONS

Separately list five to ten things that at times annoy or bug you about your spouse. Draw a line down the middle and on the other side, write out your reactions. Now talk about your responses. Pray together as a couple as you give your reactions to God.

MOSES AND THE AMALEKITES

Carry each other's burdens, and in this way you will fulfill the law of Christ.

—GALATIANS 6:2

There's a battle story in the Old Testament that has great meaning for strengthening marriages. You might not think a strategy for winning a war could draw a marriage closer, but it can.

You might know the story. A tribal people, the Amalekites, had attacked the Israelites. When Moses raised his staff toward heaven, the Israelites would begin to win the battle. But when Moses got tired and lowered the staff, the Amalekites would gain the advantage. As the battle wore on and Moses grew more tired, it looked like Israel would face defeat. But then Moses got an idea. Why not gather men around him to hold up his arms? That is exactly what happened; and with his staff raised toward heaven and others supporting his arms, Israel won.

So what's the lesson for a more intimate relationship? No one was meant to do marriage alone. No one was meant to do parenting or heartbreak alone. Life was not meant to be lived in a vacuum. We need replenishing relationships to help us hold up our staff of right priorities so we can win the battle for our marriage and family.

Cathy and I were fortunate enough to be in a couples group from our church for seven years while we raised our kids and juggled the plates of our relationship with God, each other, our children, our work, and our extended family. I first joined the group grumbling and complaining. I didn't know the people very well and I figured it would just add to my ministry demands. Cathy knew the women and came into the group with much more enthusiasm. It ended up being one of the highlights of that period of our life. Over time, just when we needed a boost or a nudge or a prayer or a word of encouragement, it came from that group.

We all have times in marriage when things aren't so great. One of the keys is to surround yourself and your marriage with people who will help in the midst of trying times. Who are the people in your life that build you up? Who speaks positively into your life? Do you invest time with these relationships on a regular basis? If you do, you know the treasure of someone coming alongside you and lifting you up. If you don't have those kinds of relationships and feel alone, don't waste another week. Seek out replenishing relationships today.

FAITH CONVERSATIONS

- Who provides a replenishing relationship to you? Talk about how they inspire or come alongside you.
- What keeps you—and us—from developing more relationships that replenish or making the existing ones deeper?

- What areas of your life could use a boost right now? How can I come alongside you more effectively?

A STEP CLOSER

REPLENISHING RELATIONSHIPS

Together create a plan to strengthen your replenishing relationships. Make three goals and put a timeline to them. (Examples: Invite a couple over for dinner; join a small group at church; meet with a possible mentor over coffee.)

Goals	**Date to Get Started**
1.	
2.	
3.	

David and Goliath

David said to the Philistine, "You come against me with sword and spear and javelin, but I come against you in the name of the Lord Almighty, the God of the armies of Israel, whom you have defied. This day the Lord will hand you over to me. . . . All those gathered here will know that it is not by sword or spear that the Lord saves; for the battle is the Lord's."

—1 Samuel 17:45, 47
(1 Samuel 17 tells the whole story.)

People of all ages love the story of David and Goliath. Neither Jim nor I went to church much until our teen years, but we already knew the incredible story. Let us put it into our own words:

The Israelites were camped out on one hill and the Philistines were on another across the valley. In a standoff that would last forty days, the only "action" came when the Philistines each day sent out their big gun, Goliath, who shouted at the Israelites and mocked their God. Goliath, of course, was a nine-foot-plus giant of a man who scared the living daylights out of pretty much everybody. Goliath wanted the Israelites to send one man to fight him. His proposition was really pretty simple. If Goliath won the battle, the Israelites would become slaves of the Philistines. If someone from Israel won, the Philistines would become their slaves. One problem, though: Israel was fresh out of giants, and as one of the modern versions of the Bible says, "The Israelites were paralyzed with fear."

As the stalemate wore on, Jesse sent his youngest son, David, to check up on his brothers who were in the army. David was a shepherd boy who played the harp. (Harpists typically don't fight giants.) David witnessed what was taking place with Goliath and immediately volunteered to fight him. David was either the bravest or most naïve person in all Israel. Nevertheless, King Saul and the other leaders listened to what he had to say: "I have wrestled bears and lions. With God's help, I am not afraid." The Israeli leadership must have wanted to get something started and they were out of ideas, so they took David up on his offer. Saul gave David his personal armor, but after struggling to even walk in it, David took off the armor, picked up five smooth stones for his sling, and started hiking down the hill toward Goliath. Goliath's response was to be expected. He laughed and mocked, and prepared to slice David to pieces.

The Israelites looked on, paralyzed with fear. Most likely the Philistines were already breaking out the choicest Philistine champagne to celebrate their victory over Israel. But notice David's attitude and whose help he needed. While the other Israelites looked at Goliath and said, "He is so big, we can't win!" David basically said, "With God's help, He is so big, I CAN'T MISS."

And with one stone David sent Goliath to his early and extra large grave.

Why is it that so many marriages fail or fall into a boring businesslike relationship? We think it's because couples don't intentionally bring God into their marriages. We are the first to admit that without our faith in God, we probably would not be married. The right kind of marriage is not one of two hearts and two minds and even two souls; it is a marriage of three, with God being placed on the throne of your marriage. This isn't about some hocus-pocus experience as much as it is developing the self-discipline and courage to bring Christ into the presence of your everyday marriage relationship.

With so many potential challenges, the odds are against couples building an intimate marriage today. Like the Israelites in Goliath's time, it's easy to become paralyzed with fear, and to stop doing what you know would create intimacy. The issues are just too big. But instead, we need to take a page out of David's playbook. With God's help, nothing in your relationship is insurmountable. With His help you can win the battle for a healthy and loving marriage.

FAITH CONVERSATIONS

- What can we do as a couple (besides going through this book together) to bring God's presence deeper into our relationship?
- Sometimes anger, bitterness, and lack of forgiveness can cause couples to draw away from God. What can we do to work on these areas of our relationship and draw closer to God and to each other?
- Who in our life might be able to help us grow spiritually together?

A STEP CLOSER

THE DAVID RESPONSE

Make a list below of any Goliath-sized issues in your relationship. (Keep it to five or six and try to agree on them.) Next to the issues, write out the "David response." You might want to close this exercise by praying together for a right attitude and for God's presence in your marriage.

Goliath-Sized Issues in Our Relationship	The David Response
1.	
2.	
3.	
4.	
5.	
6.	

Closer to God, Closer to Each Other

To keep me from becoming conceited because of these surpassingly great revelations, there was given me a thorn in my flesh, a messenger of Satan, to torment me. Three times I pleaded with the Lord to take it away from me. But he said to me, "My grace is sufficient for you, for my power is made perfect in weakness." Therefore I will boast all the more gladly about my weaknesses, so that Christ's power may rest on me.

—2 Corinthians 12:7–9

Seasons of difficulty can do two things to married couples: Draw them closer to God and each other, or tear them apart and away from God. Your response to tough times really is a choice.

Our daughter Heidi was born with a major heart complication. With little time to waste, we needed to travel from California to Boston, where she would be the one hundredth baby in the world to have a certain kind of surgery. As we were preparing to take our day-old daughter on the air ambulance, a social worker briskly walked into the hospital room, handed us her business card, and announced, "Eighty-five percent of couples who have babies with these kinds of complications end up divorced." Her bedside manner was shocking, to say the least, but we later realized how difficult life could be with a sick child. However, we decided then and there that no matter what, this new season in our lives would draw us closer together as well as closer to God.

Somewhere along the path of our marriage, we came across an incredible quote from the famous British preacher Charles Spurgeon. Considered one of the greatest orators ever, it is less known that Spurgeon suffered from frequent illnesses and severe bouts of depression. He was only fifty-seven when he died. The following words encourage and disturb, but they always remind us that in seasons of difficulty, it is our choice to draw closer to God and closer to each other.

> I am afraid that all the grace that I have received from my comfortable and easy times and happy hours, might almost lie on a penny. But the good that I have received from my sorrows, and pains, and grief is altogether incalculable. . . . We never have such close dealings with God as when we are in tribulation. . . . There is no cry so good as that which comes from the bottom of the mountains; no prayer half so hearty as that which comes up from the depths of the soul, through deep trials and afflictions. Hence they bring us to God, and we are happier; for that is the way to be happy—to live near God.*

Today our daughter Heidi is a healthy, athletic, and beautiful young woman. Her first year of life was an intense time for our

---

*Charles Spurgeon, *Joy in Your Life* (New Kensington, PA: Whitaker House, 2002), 30.

marriage, but we learned that in good times and in bad, we need to "live near God." Perhaps James, the brother of Jesus, said it best: "Draw near to God and he will draw near to you" (James 4:8 NASB).

FAITH CONVERSATIONS

- Thinking back to difficult situations we've experienced, do you think they drew us closer to each other or farther apart?
- When a tough time comes our way, what can we do to draw together?
- In today's Scripture, Paul talks about a mysterious "thorn in the flesh." How would you finish these sentences? "In my life, my thorn in the flesh is ______________________________."(It could be something that has brought you suffering.) And, "The best way for me to deal with this thorn in the flesh is to ______________________________."

A STEP CLOSER

THE CROSS

Draw a cross on a piece of paper—or if you have the skill and materials, make a cross from wood. On small pieces of paper, write words or phrases that describe difficult situations you face. Place (or nail) them on the cross. Then pray together and relinquish your pain and suffering to Christ, who sacrificed himself on the cross for you.

Rekindling Romance

Husbands, go all out in your love for your wives, exactly as Christ did for the church—a love marked by giving, not getting.

—Ephesians 5:25 THE MESSAGE

Many couples expect romance to just happen, but we have found that intentionality is the key to rekindling romance. In two places Scripture says, "Husbands, love your wives" (Ephesians 5:25; Colossians 3:19). It's directed to husbands, but it is the right advice for wives too. As we mentioned earlier, what's really inspiring is that in the original Greek wording, the meaning is closer to "keep on loving your wife," or "keep on treasuring your wife."

When the stress of life gets in the way of our romance, Cathy proactively applies what she calls the Three Golden Rules for Romance.

Make it beautiful. It's hard to hold on to negative feelings in the grandeur of nature. Beauty almost always reduces stress and allows us to get past our petty problems. Beauty reminds us that God created the universe in part for our pleasure. We are writing this devotional from one of the most beautiful spots on the planet, Napili Bay, Maui. It has been a place for us to rejuvenate our love for each other and our love for God. It has brought closeness to our marriage and our family. Obviously, a couple doesn't have to travel 2,500 miles to find beauty. It can be found in a park, on a mountain, in a garden, or anywhere that brings beauty alive for you as a couple.

Make it new. Adrenaline makes the heart grow fonder, so create interest by changing things up. Choose an activity that requires teamwork and togetherness. Just this morning we took a hike together and visited a new spot. Even when it comes to sexuality, a new and fresh experience can bring life to something that we would have never thought could become mundane. The act of doing something new together creates a bond and makes the moment feel charged. Sure it takes some intentionality, but that is part of what rekindles romance.

Make it interesting. Communication is one of the keys to romance, sexuality, and relationships. Catch a foreign film, read a book, or take a class together. We like to go on short road trips and explore new places. Anything that gives you new material to discuss and ponder is going to be good to rekindle the flame. The couples who quit developing common interests are the ones who begin to feel that their relationship is stale. Friends of ours took a ballroom dancing class and it was a spark that brought them closer. Work at rekindling the romance. For most couples the embers are burning. They just need some attention now and then.

FAITH CONVERSATIONS

- What experiences in the past have rekindled romance for you?
- What is missing from our romantic life right now?
- Of the Three Golden Rules of Romance, which one do you think we need in our relationship?

A STEP CLOSER

THE REKINDLING ROMANCE EXPERIENCE

Together plan a day or longer that will incorporate all Three Golden Rules for Romance. Look at your schedules and set a date for you to accomplish this. (Typically, to rekindle romance you don't need to have all three of these experiences, but this is your "supercharged" time to accomplish all three.)

- Make it beautiful. ______________________________
- Make it new. ___________________________________
- Make it interesting. ____________________________
- Date for this to happen: _________________________

Creating Connection

Submit to one another out of reverence for Christ.

—Ephesians 5:21

Most marriages that die do so in small increments. It's not always the big things like adultery or addictive behaviors. Sometimes we kill relationships by deciding to pay more attention to the Internet, TV, our careers, or even our children than to each other. Time together is spent talking about the kids' homework or insurance or home improvements—subjects that usually don't bring couples closer together.

Connections die if we don't consider our partner with the big decisions, and we deal a relational death blow if we don't focus on our spouse and have regular date nights, for example. If marriage is important, then we must pay attention to the marriage and take time to nurture it. When Cathy and I looked at dry spells in our relationship, it was almost always when we began to neglect the basics of connection in our marriage.

One of our friends and mentors for marriage is Dr. Dave Stoop.* At a marriage conference we participated in recently, Dave said, "Love is a continual process of seeking and losing emotional connection and then reaching out and finding it again. It is a living thing, and if we don't attend to it, it begins to atrophy." Nobody told us before marriage that it was going to take so much work to keep the fires burning in our relationship. Creating connectivity in a relationship is so much more about emotional connection than sexuality. Emotional connection centers on trust and security. Trust and security come from being willing to invest time and energy in your relationship.

We have found that couples who are connected tend to talk about their relationship. They bring up both the positives and the negatives. They give up the need to be right all the time. Trust comes from yielding to the other person's feelings and thoughts. Connection also comes from nonsexual touch. Some authorities say it takes eight to ten meaningful touches a day for a couple to thrive. It's often the little things that bring connection.

Too many couples ignore nurturing their relationship. They drift from the basics, and then one day they realize they have lost the connection. Remember that your love relationship is an active, living organism that needs to be fed and nurtured to stay healthy. As a physical therapist once told us, "I can tell you what to do to bring strength and health to your life; I can't do the work to make it happen for you."

---

*Dr. Dave Stoop is a marriage and family therapist who, along with his wife, Jan, has written several great marriage books, such as *Forgiving the Unforgivable; Just Us: Finding Intimacy with God and Each Other;* and *When Couples Pray Together: Creating Intimacy and Spiritual Wholeness.*

FAITH CONVERSATIONS

- How would you finish this sentence? "I feel most connected to you when you ______________________________."
- And this one: "I feel least connected to you when ________ ____________________."
- What can we do to nurture our relationship more effectively?

A STEP CLOSER

A PRESCRIPTION FOR CONNECTION

Together write out a prescription for closeness and connection. What can you do as a couple to nurture more connection in your relationship? As you follow your prescription, review how you are doing on a regular basis and adjust accordingly. Most people know what their marriage needs, but they don't always make the necessary changes.

The Prayer Challenge

The earnest prayer of a righteous person has great power and produces wonderful results.

—James 5:16 NLT

With the divorce rate skyrocketing even among Christians, there is hope: *Pray together.* Dr. Dave Stoop tells us that one-tenth of one percent of couples who pray together daily will get a divorce. That incredible statistic underlies what Norman Vincent Peale, the well-known pastor from New York City, used to say: "I have never met a couple who prayed together who didn't stay together." Sadly, we know a great number of people who have gotten divorced for one reason or another. But we can't think of one couple among them who said they prayed together every day.

Prayer just may be the glue that keeps a marriage strong. Yet most couples tell us that praying and growing spiritually together is the least developed part of their life as a couple. Only 4 percent of Christian couples pray together, Dr. Stoop estimates.

We want to issue a challenge to you: Pray together for your marriage each day for sixty days. If sixty days seems too long, commit to thirty. Experts say you can create a habit by simply doing the same thing over and over again for just a few weeks. Just think. If only once a day you took your spouse's hands and simply acknowledged God's presence in your relationship and family, if you offered Him praise, thanksgiving, and supplication, you would be doing more than most couples, and you would be working on your spiritual relationship at the same time. We aren't being legalistic here—no one will be tracking your commitment—but we believe that regularly praying together will benefit your marriage for a lifetime.

Will there be days you don't feel like praying? Absolutely. Especially when there is tension in the air. But often what keeps us from praying together is exactly what should draw us to prayer. For many it's low-level bitterness or anger, or feeling a lack of respect for each other. Prayer becomes the tie that binds a couple together. Prayer inspires right priorities. And as the great church father Chrysostom wrote, prayer "is the root, the fountain, the mother of a thousand blessings." Indeed, James 4:8 expresses a beautiful promise: "Come near to God and he will come near to you." This promise is certainly true for marriage relationships too.

We want to encourage you to take this sixty-day prayer challenge. It will take some discipline. But we agree with the wonderful prayer warrior of another generation, Corrie ten Boom, who said, "Don't pray when you feel like it. Have an appointment with the Lord and keep it." We hope you will take the challenge.

FAITH CONVERSATIONS

- What do you think keeps us from praying together?
- How has prayer affected our relationship for the better?
- How can I be more of a spiritual encouragement to you?

A STEP CLOSER

TAKE THE PRAYER CHALLENGE!

Will you commit to praying together for the next sixty days? Your action step is to begin right now. As Corrie ten Boom suggested, make an appointment with God.

- When is the best time?
- Where is the best place?
- How many minutes a day can we commit to this prayer challenge?

Too Busy

In six days the Lord made the heavens and the earth, and on the seventh day He rested and was refreshed.

—Exodus 31:17 NKJV

Years ago we were blessed to take family vacations in Palm Desert, California, and stay at a friend's second home. One activity our girls loved most was sitting in the spa pool in the early evening. They loved the hot jets of water moving against their backs. (So did we!) Jim was usually first in the spa—men's swimsuits apparently require less time to put on. Anyway, one time Jim noticed that the spa was incredibly dirty. The weather had been windy and there was a lot of debris in the water. Jim had two choices. He could clean out the spa or just turn on the jets and let them stir up the water and "hide" the debris. Jim took the easy way out and just turned on the jets! As the family sat in the spa enjoying the time, Jim was the only one who knew how filthy the water was—until the jets stopped, that is.

Many couples live their lives like that spa experience. Because of the busyness and pace of daily life, we can't see the "junk" building up in our lives. If we stopped long enough to look around, to consider things, of course we would notice the debris. As long as we are busy, though, we just don't feel we have the time to deal with it.

A friend of ours once told us, "If the devil can't make you bad, he will make you busy." If we don't slow down and deal with the junk in our life, relationships will begin to break down. We know a man who works eighty hours a week and is active in his church as well. We also know that his busyness is hiding a poor marriage and pain wedged deep within his soul.

Do the jets of your life just keep pumping faster and faster? Are you afraid that if you stop and slow down things will crash all around you? If so, then you are already in need of some life surgery. We suggest that you and your spouse immediately talk about cutting back and slowing the process down. When we can't find solitude and rest, we will never figure out how to live a healthy lifestyle and draw closer in our marriage. Crazy-busy lifestyles usually mean we are running from some dirt. The answer is to slow it down enough to do the work of cleaning up the debris in your life, and in doing so you will create a better life for yourself, your spouse, and your family.

FAITH CONVERSATIONS

- If you were to take your own "personal busyness temperature," how would you rate your pace of life?
- Do you think busyness is affecting our relationship? How so?

- The unbalanced life is never kind to the areas we neglect. What areas of our lives are we neglecting right now that may need some attention?

A STEP CLOSER

A FORCED SABBATICAL

Decide when would be the soonest time, as a couple, that you could take a short sabbatical (Sabbath literally means "to rest") for reflection, rest, refreshment, restoration, and recreation. A good sabbatical should be at least twenty-four hours, and it would be best if you included most of the elements above. So pull out the calendar and plan it now.

Solitude and People

Very early in the morning, while it was still dark, Jesus got up, left the house and went off to a solitary place, where he prayed.

—Mark 1:35

We heard a pastor once share a wonderful illustration about the life of Jesus and how we can live more effectively. It was all based on Luke 6, starting with verse 12, which talks about Jesus finding a place of solitude to pray. Then he came back and spent quality time with his disciples. He was ready for a busy day of ministry. As the pastor retold this story, he held up a wagon wheel and referred to the center of the wheel as *solitude*, the spokes as community or what we call *replenishing relationships*, and the wheelbase as our *vocation*. The poignant message was that for an effective life we need all three areas to be functioning together: solitude and replenishing relationships, as well as our work and family life. The illustration really hit home with us, because at that time we were putting a majority of our efforts into our work and were slacking in the areas of solitude and replenishing relationships.

The spiritual discipline of solitude and stillness has been lost in the twenty-first century. We hear people almost boast about how busy they are as though it were an indication of success. But it is in solitude where we often hear the voice of God whisper, *"You are my beloved. You are the apple of my eye."* It is in solitude that we draw upon God's strength to do what is right in our marriage or gain understanding and guidance for direction. At the same time, two types of people are vying for our attention. The louder voice is usually that of the VDPs (Very Draining People), and everyone knows some of these. But it is the VIPs (Very Inspiring People) who replenish us.

We are sure you can name people who build you up and energize you when you are in their presence. You feel better for having spent time with them. Just this week we had dinner with Dale and Karen, who are two of our VIPs. Do you proactively invest regular time with inspiring people? Your life and marriage will be better for it. After building into your life the priority of solitude and replenishing relationships, you will be ready to tackle your work, ministry, and marriage. You can't short-cut the process; our bodies and spirits were meant to be revived by times of solitude and healthy relationships.

FAITH CONVERSATIONS

- How would you describe your solitude time with God?
- Are you happy with the replenishing friendships you have, as well as the ones we have as a couple? Do you wish they were deeper?

- On a scale of 1 to 10, how would you rank your work and family life? (1 being "needs immediate attention" and 10 representing "excellent.")

A STEP CLOSER

SOLITUDE—RELATIONSHIPS—VOCATION

Here or on a separate piece of paper, write out your goals related to solitude, replenishing relationships, and work or ministry that you have individually and as a couple.

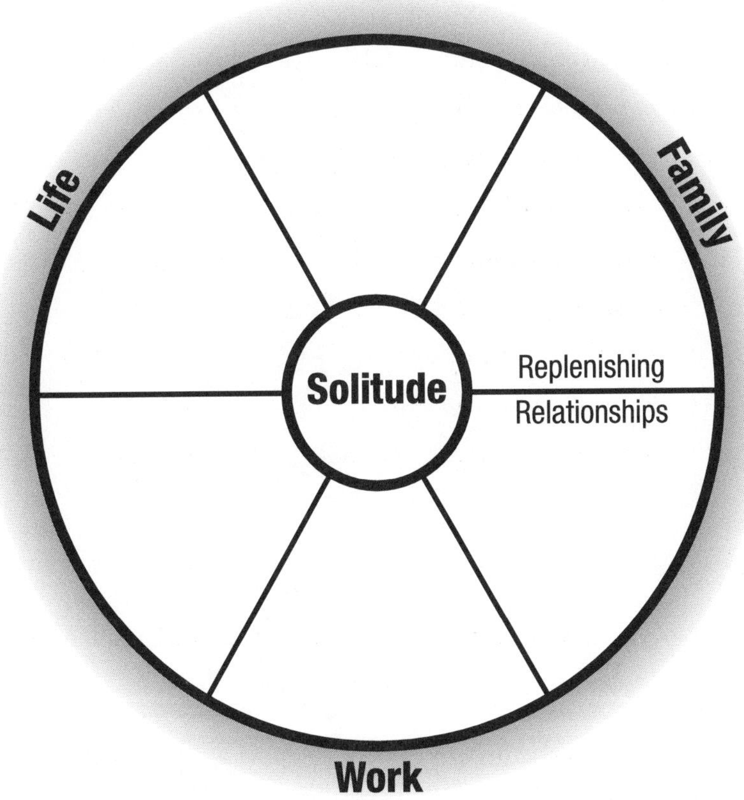

Weekly Meetings

Let us think of ways to motivate one another to acts of love and good works. And let us not neglect our meeting together, as some people do, but encourage one another. . . .

—Hebrews 10:24–25 NLT

Some people dread meetings. But in a marriage, we think three types of weekly meetings can help a relationship grow more than you might imagine: a regular date with each other, a business meeting to tackle the family needs, and a time to grow spiritually together. You may not actually call them meetings, but we have never had a couple try our experiment and not say it was helpful. Yes, life is busy. Work and children can take lots of time and energy, but that is exactly why we believe three intentional meetings with your spouse each week can do wonders for your relationship.

The nonnegotiable date. Earlier in this book we talked about nonnegotiable dates (see page 27), so hopefully you already are having a date each week where you are focusing on each other and spicing up the romance. Spontaneity is great, but romance often takes intentionality, so make your date a sacred part of your schedule. The date doesn't have to be expensive, and if you have kids, you can always trade baby-sitting with another couple. Your kids won't miss you, and actually, it will give them a sense of security and a role model to see that their mom and dad still court each other. It may not be healthy for them or for you if your kids think they are the center of your universe. A weekly date is good for everyone.

The business meeting. With or without kids, life together can resemble a family business. There are bills to be paid, decisions to be made about insurance, home improvements, and how time is spent in and out of the home. We have found that many of those decisions can be made in a weekly meeting that takes less than an hour. Hey, splurge and have the meeting over a grande Frappuccino instead of late at night when you are both too tired to really care about the issues to be discussed. Our personal testimony is that we don't do well late at night dealing with money, schedules, kids' homework, or when the relatives are coming to visit. When family business issues are brought up in between meetings, we simply ask each other, "Can it wait until the business meeting?" Usually it can, and the meeting actually gets us in the mood to handle that kind of stuff.

The spiritual growth time. By now you have figured it out: It's important to set a time to grow together spiritually. We must confess that this devotional comes out of our many times of trying every devotional experience known to humankind and mostly failing. Finally we felt the freedom to meet only once a week. We try to pray together more often, but an intentional time of spiritual growth once a week will do wonders for your togetherness. If you already do it more often, please keep it up. If not, start a weekly meeting and add more if you want to. We find the best experience is to schedule this time when there are few distractions. And because it can be easy to postpone, we have an appointment to make it happen. You can keep the time short, but try to incorporate inspiration, sharing, and prayer. Those three ingredients make for a great time of growth spiritually. And if your time falls at a moment when you are having some difficulties, do it anyway. Who knows? With God's help you may just be able to turn a corner in your relationship.

Today's Scripture from Hebrews is really meant for the church and not for couples per se, but if you read it again, the truth found in it for a marriage is incredibly powerful. A nurturing, loving relationship is often spelled T-I-M-E, so don't neglect meeting together. Our experience is that if you don't put it on the calendar, it won't happen.

FAITH CONVERSATIONS

- How do you feel about the suggestion to have three meetings a week?
- Which of the three meetings do we do best, and which could use some improvement?
- How do you think the words in Scripture for today apply to our life?

A STEP CLOSER

THREE MEETINGS A WEEK

You probably already know where this action step will take you. We are suggesting that if you don't already have three meetings scheduled that you at least try it. Pull out your calendar and write in the time and place for each week of the month.

Nonnegotiable Date	**Business Meeting**	**Spiritual Growth Time**
1.	1.	1.
2.	2.	2.
3.	3.	3.
4.	4.	4.

Conflict Can Bring You Closer, Or...

Make a clean break with all cutting, backbiting, profane talk. Be gentle with one another, sensitive. Forgive one another as quickly and thoroughly as God in Christ forgave you.

—Ephesians 4:31–32 The Message

We saw this sign in a flower shop in Florida:

> Two Secrets to Keeping Your Marriage Brimming . . .
> Whenever you are wrong, admit it.
> Whenever you are right, shut up.

Actually, that's not bad advice. No matter how you respond, though, conflict in a relationship is inevitable. But conflict doesn't need to pull you apart. This may sound crazy, but conflict can bring you closer. It can even be good for your relationship. And making up isn't half bad either.

The issue with most couples is not how much conflict there is, but how they deal with it. No one, and we mean no one, can agree on every issue. And that is just as true for Christian couples. When we were younger a couple told us Christians should never argue. (That couple later divorced.)

Just as sports have rules, couples should have rules in order to have healthy conflict.

Choose your battles wisely. Don't turn every discussion into a fight. If you do enter into conflict, speak the truth in love. But not everything is worth fighting over. Does it really matter if the house is kept in perfect order? It's impossible to have a fun-loving relationship if you are managing too many battlefronts at one time. Sometimes a compromise is the wisest decision. Your relationship is a lot like your bank account. It takes more deposits than withdrawals to get a good report.

Keep anger under control. When a sinner marries another sinner and later "sinnerlings" are added to the mix, there are bound to be times when you will get angry with your spouse. Anger isn't the issue; it's keeping it in control and handling it with maturity and grace. We find that people who harbor a lot of anger usually have other issues going on in their life. Put limits on your anger so it doesn't turn to bitterness and resentment. Anger that is held on the inside is often more detrimental than expressed anger. If you hold grudges or keep the flames of anger burning for too long, you are going against these scriptural mandates: "Don't sin by letting anger control you." "Don't let the sun go down while you are still angry, for anger gives a foothold to the devil." "Get rid of all bitterness, rage, anger, harsh words, and slander, as well as all types of evil behavior." In other words, we can be angry but not sin. This takes some strong self-control, but the self-discipline will draw you closer.

Practice forgiveness. Conflict is inevitable, but you can choose forgiveness. Words like "I'm sorry, will you forgive me?" and "I love you and forgive you" will draw you closer to each other. God practices a severe mercy and an extravagant grace. Grace literally means unmerited favor. If God bestows grace on you, wouldn't it seem a bit arrogant not to bestow grace on your spouse? Though conflict is inevitable, how you deal with the conflict will be the determining factor in the strength of your relationship.

FAITH CONVERSATIONS

- What do you think about how we deal with conflict?
- Do you think we have issues about choosing battles? Keeping anger under control? Practicing forgiveness?
- What could we do to practice not letting the sun go down on our anger?

A STEP CLOSER

THE FORGIVENESS FACTOR

Choose a time when you can be in a quiet place for a while to talk. Then walk through some of your past conflicts and offenses with each other and ask for forgiveness. Close this session by praying together. We have found that this can be a very powerful time. (Do not hesitate to seek the help of a counselor or pastor if your issues are bigger than you can handle.)

A High-Maintenance Marriage

Being confident of this, that he who began a good work in you will carry it on to completion until the day of Christ Jesus.

—Philippians 1:6

We have often said publicly that we have a high-maintenance marriage. We have been married for over thirty-five years, and we feel a bit like how Billy Graham described his fifty-four-year marriage: "Ruth and I are happily incompatible." Cathy and I wouldn't trade our relationship for anything, but it hasn't always been easy. It's kind of like what Rocky Balboa said to his wife in the famous movie *Rocky*: "I got gaps; you got gaps; we fill each other's gaps."

For twenty-five years we have lived next door to Bill, who has the coolest Corvette Stingray roadster. It is a beautiful car and fun to drive. Okay, he has never actually let me drive it—but I know it would be fun if I did! Bill spends a great deal of time, energy, and money to keep his high-performance machine in good shape. It needs regular oil changes and all the other maintenance cars need to keep it beautiful and in running order. If he ignored that car, it would eventually break down and just quit working.

In differing degrees, marriages are high maintenance with at least a bit of incompatibility mixed in them. But that doesn't stop the good marriages from being even better, and there is hope for even the most difficult relationships. What does it take to make a high-maintenance marriage successful? One word: *work.* The best marriages are the ones where both parties are willing to work at it on a regular basis.

Marriage expert Willard Harley told us on the *HomeWord* radio broadcast that almost any marriage can succeed if the couple is willing to invest the time. How much time? He said fifteen to twenty hours a week. Now, that is a lot of time to add to an already overcrowded schedule. But if your marriage is a bit high maintenance, what are your other options? Of marriages that end in divorce, the average first marriage in America lasts seven years, and the average second marriage lasts four. Personally, we would rather work on the first one and do all we can to make it better. Regardless of your history, today is the day to choose to make your marriage better. And this is your promise from the Bible: "[God,] who began a good work in you will carry it on to completion."

Here is our list of five things every couple can do to invest in their marriage. None of these is rocket science and they all take work. Our experience is that it is definitely worth it.

Talk. Communicate on a deeper level daily, if possible. Take a walk. Sit together on the couch for fifteen minutes after dinner, even if there is chaos all around you. You can't grow together if you don't talk.

Show affection. Authorities on the subject tell us that it takes eight to ten meaningful touches a day for a person to thrive. Showering your spouse with affection is one of the best ways to keep the sparks flowing. (Men, we aren't talking about groping!) Women often say that non-sexual affection is even more powerful.

Walk. This may sound corny, but couples who walk together talk together. We find that when we put a leash on the dog and walk around the block, we end up having good conversations.

Express kindness. Random acts of kindness go a long way in a high-maintenance marriage. A nice card or running an errand for your spouse may do more for your relationship than many other things.

Pray. Couples who pray together, stay together. We have said before that without God's presence in our marriage, we would probably not be married today. The odds would be against us. We like what Paul said: "I can do everything through him who gives me strength" (Philippians 4:13). That statement goes for marriage as well.

Leo Tolstoy was not necessarily known as a marriage expert, but he was so right when he said, "What counts in making a marriage happy is not so much how compatible you are but how you deal with your incompatibility." Good thoughts, Leo.

FAITH CONVERSATIONS

- Do you think our marriage is high maintenance, low maintenance, or somewhere in between?
- What is the one thing you think our marriage needs more of?
- Is there something our marriage needs less of?

A STEP CLOSER

CHERISHING DAYS

Marriage expert Norm Wright challenges couples to try a Cherishing Day exercise, where each partner makes a list of simple cherishing behaviors he/she would enjoy receiving from the other.

- Make them specific and positive
- Do not involve past conflicts or old demands
- Do them on a regular basis
- Achieve them with little time or expense

Individually make a list of at least five experiences and share them with each other.

Physical Intimacy

The husband should fulfill his wife's sexual needs, and the wife should fulfill her husband's needs. The wife gives authority over her body to her husband, and the husband gives authority of his body to his wife.

—1 Corinthians 7:3–4 NLT

With so much emphasis on sex and sexuality in today's culture, you might be surprised to know that most couples have times when they struggle with physical intimacy. If there is little emotional intimacy in a marriage relationship, you probably won't have much quality physical intimacy. "I'm too tired" is usually an indication that priorities are in the wrong place and things need to be discussed. Bob had to be honest with Janet and tell her that his workaholic tendencies had cheated her out of getting his very best when it came to meeting some of her needs in the romance department. Jennifer was so busy with the kids and her part-time business that she finally admitted to her husband that she had cheated him out of what had once been a very vibrant and active physical relationship.

Gary and Barb Rosberg are two of our favorite marriage experts. In their book *The Five Sex Needs of Men and Women,** they provide some helpful insights:

Men Need	**Women Need**
1. Mutual satisfaction	1. Affirmation
2. Communication	2. Communication
3. Responsiveness of wife	3. Non-sexual touch
4. Initiation of wife	4. Spiritual intimacy
5. Affirmation	5. Romance

For both husbands and wives, intimacy is much more than physical. It is only after your hearts meet that your bodies will meet in the best of ways.

Jesus quoted the Old Testament, saying, "Haven't you read in your Bible that the Creator originally made man and woman for each other, male and female? And because of this, a man leaves father and mother and is firmly bonded to his wife, becoming one flesh—no longer two bodies but one. Because God created this organic union of the two sexes, no one should desecrate his art by cutting them apart" (Matthew 19:4–6 The Message). To become one with our spouse means we first have to become one with our emotional connections. Meet each other's emotional and relational needs, and the physical needs will follow suit.

*Gary and Barbara Rosberg, *The Five Sex Needs of Men and Women* (Carol Stream, IL: Tyndale House, 2006), 40.

FAITH CONVERSATIONS

- What type of emotional connection would you want from me that would enhance our physical intimacy?"
- Many couples have trouble talking about physical intimacy. On a scale of 1 to 5 (1 being poor and 5 being great), how would you rank our ability to talk about sexual intimacy?
- Review the five sex needs of men and women. Did any surprise you?

A STEP CLOSER

OUR PHYSICAL INTIMACY NEEDS

When couples talk about their physical/sexual needs, it draws them closer to each other. Make a list of your top five sex needs and wants as a husband and as a wife and then talk about them.

Husband's sex needs and wants	Wife's sex needs and wants
1.	1.
2.	2.
3.	3.
4.	4.
5.	5.

Strategic Romance

While the king was at his table, my perfume spread its fragrance. My lover is to me a sachet of myrrh resting between my breasts. My lover is to me a cluster of henna blossoms from the vineyards of En Gedi. How beautiful you are, my darling! Oh, how beautiful! Your eyes are doves. How handsome you are, my lover! Oh, how charming! And our bed is verdant.

—Song of Songs 1:12–16

Someone once told us that romance is easy. All I had to do was surprise my wife with a simple gift like flowers and then plan a surprise experience, something small but nice, like a picnic dinner or something more involved, like taking her away for a night after packing her clothes, taking care of the kids' needs, and picking her up at work.

We think this guy understood romance better than most. He knew that first and foremost romance is not about sex. It's about intentionality and action. And beautiful sexuality comes after romance. Gary and Barb Rosberg said it so well: "Love is a feeling; romance is love in action."*

Almost all healthy couples will respond to simple displays of romance like bringing home flowers or a loving card when it is unexpected. Taking time away on an afternoon for a leisurely walk together, love notes, a surprise getaway, romantic music, creating a home-spa environment with candles and soft lights—these are all ways of doing what some would call "strategic romance." These romantic ideas don't cost much, but they do take just a bit of intentionality. Too often romance is blocked by distractions like financial issues, lack of time or creativity, chores to do, kids' activities, and a host of other everyday things. But it doesn't have to be that way.

Solomon (in the Old Testament) was the all-time romantic. If you haven't read the book Song of Songs (or Song of Solomon) in the Bible for a while, or ever for that matter, take a look. You'll get some great romantic ideas—even in the first chapter.

Kiss. "Let him kiss me with the kisses of his mouth—for your love is more delightful than wine" (Song of Songs 1:2). Do you kiss with love and passion? A prostitute once said, "I will make love with my clients, but I won't kiss them. That's way too intimate." Soft and romantic kissing is often a sign of how your relationship is doing. If it is lacking, most likely other parts of your romantic life are lacking as well.

Take time to clean up and enjoy each other. "Pleasing is the fragrance of your perfumes; your name is like perfume poured out. . . . Take me away with you" (Song of Songs 1:3, 4). In the

---

*Rosberg, *The Five Sex Needs of Men and Women,* 124.

first chapter of Song of Songs, Solomon's wife is pouring it on. She compliments him on how he smells, she praises him, she initiates with the words: "Take me away. . . . Let the king bring me into his chambers." This type of flirting and the time it takes to enjoy each other is incredibly romantic. When was the last time you took time to be proactive in the romance department? If it has been a while, plan something, and you will experience the benefits of preparation.

Create an En Gedi experience. "My lover is to me a cluster of henna blossoms from the vineyards of En Gedi" (Song of Songs 1:14). En Gedi is an incredible oasis in the middle of the desert. David hid out with his men in the caves of En Gedi. In Israel, En Gedi is an oasis for travelers to stop by the waterfall, enjoy the birds, flowers, and quiet directly off the road in the barren desert. In the first chapter of the Song of Songs, Solomon and his wife give each other the romantic gifts of affirmation and special presents. With words and intentionality they basically seduce each other by creating an oasis of safety and refuge in the midst of their home. Is your marriage a place of safety and refuge? It can be with some strategic romance added to your relationship.

FAITH CONVERSATIONS

- What do you wish I would give to you when it comes to romance?
- How could we build En Gedi experiences in our relationship? (If you need help, read the first chapter of the Song of Songs.)
- What keeps us from being more romantic with each other?

A STEP CLOSER

EN GEDI EXPERIENCE

Create a romantic experience together. The element of surprise is often a wonderful way to produce more romance. However, it is also great to plan a romantic experience together and look forward to it. Discuss elements of how you will go about creating an oasis experience in the midst of your busy lives. Plan it. Prepare for it. Enjoy.

Stop Complaining, Start Enjoying

Do everything without complaining or arguing, so that you may become blameless and pure, children of God without fault in a crooked and depraved generation, in which you shine like stars in the universe.

—Philippians 2:14–15

We love the plaque on a friend's kitchen wall that says "I complained because I had no shoes until I met a man who had no feet." Every time we walk into that kitchen we are reminded that we spend too much of our time complaining and grumbling about things that really don't matter. Complaining is just a bad, bad habit. Constant complaining and criticism shut down marital intimacy. Plus, complainers and grumblers are unhappy people.

Will Bowen recently wrote a bestselling book called *A Complaint-Free World*. He challenges his readers to stop complaining for twenty-one consecutive days. It has been said that's how long it takes to break a habit. Chronic complainers may need a few more days than twenty-one to break their vicious cycle of unhappiness. Complaining traps you in a constant state of feeling like something is wrong.

A woman came up to us at a Ministry and Marriage seminar we were giving. She pointed to her husband, who was holding their baby. She said, "Our relationship changed for the better when I quit complaining and changed my expectations." She told us her story: "I was always disappointed with my husband. He never met my expectations. One day I realized I expected him to be my best friend, passionate lover, counselor, perfect dad, handyman, spiritual leader, and provider, and I expected him to get in better physical shape. I had imagined a relationship that was basically out of a romance novel. I complained to an older woman at my church about my husband, who happened to be the pastor of the church."

The woman, who had become somewhat of a mentor to the younger woman, said, "Does your husband come home sober from work? Is he engaged with your children? Has he been faithful to your wedding vows? Does he have a steady job? He doesn't appear to be an extreme athlete, but does he take care of his body most of the time? Does he do the best he can?" I had to answer yes to those questions. She interrupted me before I could finish "But he doesn't—" She smiled and said, "I would simply shut up about all he is not doing or being and praise him for what he does. The person who may need to change in the relationship is you." The older woman quoted a famous verse from a modern-day poet:

> If you don't like it, change it.
> If you can't change it, change your attitude.
> Don't complain.*

---

*Maya Angelou, *Wouldn't Take Nothing for My Journey Now* (New York: Bantam Books, 1994), 87.

If you find yourself complaining about your spouse or your place in life, maybe you are the one who needs to change first. Even one step in the right direction away from complaining and toward affirmation will do wonders for your relationship.

FAITH CONVERSATIONS

- Does our relationship have too much negativity and complaining in it?
- What can we do about not taking each other for granted and affirming each other more often?
- How can I learn from the experience of the woman who wanted her husband to be all things to her?

A STEP CLOSER

THE NO-COMPLAINT CHALLENGE

Try your best not to complain for a full week. You can't repress all the problems of your life, but for a week you can free yourself from verbalizing them. Check back with each other after a week and report how you did and how it felt. You may want to put today's verse in a highly visible place to remind you to stop complaining and start enjoying life.

Do Your Kids a Favor: Love Your Spouse

May your fountain be blessed, and may you rejoice in the wife of your youth. A loving doe, a graceful deer . . . may you ever be captivated by her love.

—Proverbs 5:18–19

Some couples have a difficult time putting their marriage relationship ahead of raising their children in order of priority. (Even if you don't have children yet, keep reading!) It's easy to fall into a child-focused marriage, and usually the marriage relationship suffers when kids are almost always put first. We think your greatest family investment is your marriage. Obviously, this doesn't mean you leave the kids to fend for themselves. They may need more focused time at various stages in their development, but happy and fulfilled kids come from families where they feel secure in their parents' relationship with each other.

The most important thing a father can do for his children is to love their mother and vice versa. Here's what Leonard Sweet says about the subject: "The more a marriage is spirited and sporting, the better off the kids. It's impossible to have a healthy family without a healthy marriage. One of the best gifts parents can bequeath to children is the example of two people in love bound together in a vibrant covenant relationship."* Frankly, this has been a struggle for us. We have tended to put much of our time and energy into the lives of our children, and there were seasons in our marriage when we were much more focused on the kids than on each other. It's easy to do. The kids are constantly needy and as adults we seem to get by okay with less attention. However, a loved-starved relationship breeds trouble.

A friend of ours uses the illustration of a hose with oxygen feeding your lungs. If someone steps on the hose and it shuts off the air supply, you will quickly begin to die. It's the same with a marriage relationship. Step on the hose supplying fresh air to the marriage and it will quit growing. When the kids come along, far too often it is the end of courting our mate. If couples put half the effort into their marriage that they invested in their dating life, they would be surprised at how successful the relationship would be—and how secure the kids would feel.

We have gone back to some key questions to help us draw closer together and focus on our marriage relationship as a priority. What was it we did when we were dating that drew us closer together? Are we still doing that now that there are kids in the picture? Where is my spouse in my top-five priorities? How would my spouse answer that question? There is often a significant drop in marital satisfaction,

---

*Leonard Sweet, *Soul Salsa: Seventeen Surprising Steps for Godly Living in the 21st Century* (Grand Rapids, MI: Zondervan, 2002), 204.

especially in the area of romance, when children arrive on the scene. However, the most positive marriages keep making romance a priority as well. Sure it takes some juggling. No one said it would be simple. A strong marriage will definitely take some work. However, the vitality it will bring to your entire family is worth it.

FAITH CONVERSATIONS

- How are we doing? Is our relationship more child-focused than couple-focused?
- Were my parents and your parents role models in this? How do their relationships affect us now?
- What can we do this week to tweak our relationship in order to help our children feel more secure?

A STEP CLOSER

THE PRIORITY OF MARRIAGE

List three things you can do with each other to raise the awareness in your children that marriage is a covenant gift from God. How will these things show your children how to have a healthy marriage?

1.

2.

3.

Waking Up Is a Gift

This is the day the Lord has made; let us rejoice and be glad in it.

—Psalm 118:24

We have a friend who takes people on tours to climb Mount Kilimanjaro in Tanzania, East Africa. She heard our family was going through some tough times this year, and she had no idea how much she ministered to us with her story. She told us that she had recently climbed Kilimanjaro with twelve people. One of the men stood out from the rest. No matter what they were doing—eating, working, flying, resting, walking—joy spilled out from him. Finally, after a week of being together in close proximity, our friend asked this man the secret to his joy. He told her that four years prior he had been diagnosed with cancer and given six months to live. He fought the cancer and beat it, and now every morning his thought is *Waking up is a gift.* He tries to live in the moment as much as he can.

After the climb, our friend came down with an extremely painful back. Her doctor said her choices were surgery or pain medication. She said she lost all of her energy and her hope as well. It affected every aspect of her life, including her relationship with her husband. The pain was all-encompassing. She decided not to have surgery and to refrain from medication while she did back exercises given to her by her physical therapist.

Then she remembered the inspiring man from her climb of Kilimanjaro. She decided that even in the worst of her painful days, she would see waking up as a gift. She worked on having an "attitude of gratitude." Even on bad pain days, she thanked God for the smell of the sea, the taste of a chicken tostada, a rainbow that she had seen the day before. She thanked God for her family and their support. She thanked God that no matter how bad it got, she didn't have to stay focused on the negative. Her back didn't get better immediately. But over time the pain was gone. She says the greatest miracle was not living pain-free, but learning that waking up is a gift.

Almost every day before I (Jim) get out of bed, I recite Psalm 118:24: "This is the day the Lord has made; [I will] rejoice and be glad in it." Joy is sometimes an act of the will. Problems may not change around you, but your attitude can change, and that makes all the difference. Today as you perhaps face family health problems, financial pressures, or the needy people near you, realize that waking up is a gift and that a great goal is to acknowledge the fact that God created this day to allow you to walk through it rejoicing and with Him by your side. This attitude does wonders for your marriage and your family. Today is a gift. Your spouse is a gift. Your family is a gift.

All that you have is a gift from God. He is our sustainer and provider. He gives us the gift of life.

FAITH CONVERSATIONS

- I needed to be reminded of this message today because ____.
- How does the thought *waking up is a gift* affect our marriage?
- Read today's Scripture verse again and discuss together the many powerful ways these words can affect your life and relationship.

A STEP CLOSER

THIS IS THE DAY

"This is the day the Lord has made; let us rejoice and be glad in it."

Make a list of all the things that you can rejoice in within your life, relationship, and family. Then take a few moments to thank God for all He has done in your life.

1.
2.
3.
4.
5.
6.

7.

8.

9.

10.

A Life of Significant Conversations

Jesus told her, "I am the resurrection and the life. Anyone who believes in me will live, even after dying. Everyone who lives in me and believes in me will never ever die."

—John 11:25–26 NLT

We received a letter in the mail today telling us that a good friend from several years ago, Jim Rigby, had died of cancer. We sat at the kitchen table and reflected on the times we'd spent together, usually in ministry settings, with Jim and his wonderful wife, Susan. Susan is the outgoing one. She is a real people magnet. She is fun and passionate about life with a contagious laugh. Jim, on the other hand, was quieter. He was—and we don't mean this in a negative way—simple. He did a lot more listening than talking. There was nothing complicated about Jim. We realized we had both had significant conversations with him years ago. He would just sort of slide up next to you, and you would find yourself talking to him about important stuff. The cancer gave his family the opportunity to hear from many people, even those they hadn't met, and to learn about Jim's unparalleled influence on their lives, professionally and spiritually.

When the doctor had to tell Jim his cancer was inoperable and untreatable, he said, "Mr. Rigby, I am so sorry to give you this news." But Jim's faith was so deep in God that he didn't even skip a beat when he replied, "You only need to be sorry if you believe that this life is the ultimate good." One woman he worked with said: "Other people talk a lot about being a Christian, but when I think of what a true Christian is, I think of Jim Rigby." What a tribute. What a life well lived.

In the end, it will be the significant conversations we have that will matter most. Our marriage blends two very opposite personalities. One of us is an extrovert and the other an introvert. But we both agree that actions speak louder than words. A significant conversation may be more about actions than words. Significant conversation with each other and with others has made our marriage more successful.

When was the last time you and your spouse had a significant conversation—one that brought you connection and emotional intimacy? Ours was last night, talking about Jim Rigby as we sipped tea and reflected on the brevity of life on earth as compared to eternity. The apostle John said it best: "Little children, let us not love with word or with tongue, but in deed and truth" (1 John 3:18 NASB).

FAITH CONVERSATIONS

- When was the last time we had a significant conversation?
- What times together draw out deeper connections for us as a couple?

- How does the thought of eternal life bring stronger connection with each other?

A STEP CLOSER

A WEEKLY MEETING

For years we tried every devotional out there to draw closer together. We usually started out good the first week, but then it began to slide pretty quickly. Then we came up with the idea to meet once a week and just talk. We used the same format week after week. The words below are what have helped us relate and connect. Take time either now or in the next few days to try this out. Adapt it to make it work for you. We know hundreds of couples who use this tool as a way to make significant conversation.

- *Devotional time of the week* (Start by sharing something you have learned this week from God.)
- *Greatest joy of the week* (What one part of your life this week brought you joy?)
- *Greatest struggle of the week* (What did you struggle with that you want to share?)
- *An affirmation* (Give a word of affirmation and encouragement to your spouse.)
- *A wish or a hope* (Is there one wish or hope you would like to share?)
- *Physical goals* (Do you have a goal this week related to your physical health or life?)

- *Prayers* (Take a few minutes to share prayer requests and pray for each other.)
- *Book of the month* (Is there a book or article that you may want to read together and then discuss?)

DIFFERENT BY DESIGN

Therefore, accept each other just as Christ has accepted you so that God will be given glory.

—ROMANS 15:7 NLT

Here is an actual conversation in the Jim and Cathy world as Jim sits on the extra comfy chair in the den. "Jim, what are you doing right now?" "I'm doing nothing." "Well then, what are you thinking about as you sit there?" "I'm not really thinking about anything. I'm just sitting here relaxing." (More intense and a bit irritated.) "Jim, you must be thinking about something!" "Honest, I am just sitting here not thinking about anything." Cathy finally gives up. Jim just keeps on sitting, thinking about and doing nothing.

The Bible says, "So God created human beings in his own image. In the image of God he created them; male and female he created them" (Genesis 1:27 NLT). The same creator made men and women, but they really are made differently. For many couples, what drew them to each other now bugs them. This happened for us. You have no doubt heard the statement "Men are like waffles, and women are like spaghetti." We have not yet met a woman who is not good at multitasking. She can talk on the phone, make dinner, help with homework, feed the dog, design the new marketing plan at work, and decide what she is going to wear for church tomorrow without skipping a beat. All the strands of spaghetti touch each other, and that seems to be how she lives best.

A man seems to be more like a waffle. He lives with little compartments in his head. He deals with the kids' homework, and then goes back to the business plan for work. He can talk about the family finances with his wife, but when it's over, he stores the finance facts back in their compartment and then wants to pick up on romance. There is no way she is interested in romance, because she is still juggling how they are going to pay the insurance bill on Friday.

Men even have a compartment in their head for *no words*. Women can hardly even imagine it. Roger and Ben went to a professional baseball game. They didn't talk much during the game, but did make a few comments about work and baseball. Roger's wife and Ben's wife went to the same game. They talked throughout the entire game, cheered wildly for their team, and discussed in depth Ben's upcoming surgery. Problems with kids, health, and last week's sermon were also game-time topics. When Roger's wife mentioned Ben's upcoming surgery, Roger didn't know anything about it. Both couples had a great time at the game.

So why do couples spend so much time trying to change their spouse? Don't we already know it doesn't work? The key to lasting love in your marriage is to change yourself and accept your spouse unconditionally. Nobody can change your marriage but you. You can't manage, or control, or nag your spouse to become more like you. In fact, if you really were honest you wouldn't want your spouse to be just like you. So appreciate the differences, accept the fact that you will look at life differently, and remember this: Your emotional well-being should never depend on another person's meeting your expectations.

FAITH CONVERSATIONS

- What aspects of my personality or lifestyle do you appreciate even if they are different from yours?
- What differences between us bother you the most?
- How does today's verse apply to our marriage?

A STEP CLOSER

COMPLEMENTING EACH OTHER'S STRENGTHS

Make three lists.

- First, list each other's strengths and God-given talents.
- Next to the two lists, write how you complement each other with differing gifts.
- Take some time to pray together, thanking God that you were created differently and yet your strengths mesh together to make you a couple that brings glory to God.

Husband's Strengths/ God-Given Talents	Wife's Strengths/ God-Given Talents	How We Complement Each Other

DO WHAT IT TAKES

"Therefore everyone who hears these words of mine and puts them into practice is like a wise man who built his house on the rock. The rain came down, the streams rose, and the winds blew and beat against that house; yet it did not fall, because it had its foundation on the rock. But everyone who hears these words of mine and does not put them into practice is like a foolish man who built his house on sand. The rain came down, the streams rose, and the winds blew and beat against that house, and it fell with a great crash."

—MATTHEW 7:24–27

A successful marriage is not the result of marrying the perfect person or feeling the right emotions. It's not even about thinking the right thoughts or even praying the right prayer. A successful marriage that draws you closer to each other is about doing the right things, period. David Viscott writes, "Relationships seldom die because they suddenly have no life left in them. They wither slowly, either because people do not understand how much or what kind of upkeep, time, work, love, and caring they require or because people are too lazy or afraid to try."* A successful marriage is not a gift, it's an achievement. We know love doesn't always last—you have to make it last.

The foundational component of an excellent marriage is a truly secure environment—one that is physically, intellectually, spiritually, and emotionally secure. We often ask the question "Why do some couples manage to enjoy a lasting love despite facing the same circumstances that defeat others?" We think it has to do with being willing to work on their relationship, and because they are willing to work at the issues, the relationship will find security. It's not always about resolving problems as much as it is being willing to put effort into investing in the relationship.

At the end of the Sermon on the Mount, Jesus gave a most profound illustration—He challenged people to build their house on the Rock instead of sand. He didn't promise that rain, wind, and storms would not come to them. In fact, He inferred that storms come to everyone. It is more about how we go about building our home, our life, and our marriage. If we work at building it on the Rock, there will be times when clouds form, the winds blow, and rain falls, but the sun will keep shining on your relationship as you put the energy into keeping it strong.

If you want to be closer in your marriage, it is going to take working as hard at your relationship as you do with your vocation

---

*Mark Gungor, *Laugh Your Way to a Better Marriage* (New York: Atria Books, 2008), xi.

or parenting or whatever keeps you up at night. Someone once said, "The unbalanced life is never kind to the areas we neglect." That's why the couples we know who do the best in their marital relationship are the ones that *do whatever it takes* to make it work. If it takes counseling, go to counseling. If it takes setting special date nights or reading books, do it. If it takes a daily communication appointment to keep the fires burning, do that. You have within you what it takes to create a good marriage. The question is, are you willing to do the work to make it better? As Martin Luther said so well, "There is no more lovely, friendly, and charming relationship, communion, or company than a good marriage."

FAITH CONVERSATIONS

- What areas of our marriage do we need to work on to find more intimacy and connection?
- Are there storms that keep us from drawing closer together? What are they and how can today's Scripture give us hope?
- "A successful marriage is not a gift, it is an achievement." How does this comment speak to our relationship?

A STEP CLOSER

BUILDING A STRONG FOUNDATION

Everyone knows that to build a strong home you must first start with a strong marriage. What are four foundational pillars to base your marriage on? Together come up with your four pillars and write out two ways you can together build a stronger foundation under each of your chosen pillars.

Pillar 1 __________	**Pillar 2** __________	**Pillar 2** __________	**Pillar 4** __________
1.	1.	1.	1.
2.	2.	2.	2.

THE BEST THINGS IN LIFE ARE NOT THINGS

Do not store up for yourselves treasures on earth, where moth and rust destroy, and where thieves break in and steal. But store up for yourselves treasures in heaven, where moth and rust do not destroy, and where thieves do not break in and steal. For where your treasure is, there your heart will be also.

—MATTHEW 6:19–21

There are two ongoing battles for your soul. The world's value system places emphasis on things and stuff. God's value system is focused on relationships, beauty, and stewardship. Some estimate that the root cause for the majority of divorces stems from money problems. The statistics are staggering, and the money pit is a dangerous place to live out your marriage.

The pressure to live within our means takes a toll on the institution of marriage. Money is simply a medium of exchange, but the use and misuse of it gets tangled up in emotional complexities like love, power, and self-worth. For whatever reason, most of us did not receive good training in financial matters, and it has affected our marriages because of poor stewardship, poor investment decisions, and lack of setting up healthy boundaries. Jesus made a strong statement when He said, "No one can serve two masters. For you will hate one and love the other; you will be devoted to one and despise the other. You cannot serve both God and money" (Matthew 6:24 NLT). Too many well-meaning couples serve the god of money by choice or by default.

We are not financial experts. However, we have found three basic financial principles to strengthen your marriage that we know work. They are good, sound financial advice, but better yet, when you live by these principles, your marriage will immediately be placed on more solid ground. You can live on little or much; the principles remain the same.

- *Delay Gratification.* You will have to buy into the philosophy that the best things in life are not things. Debt is slavery. If you can't pay cash for the new bicycles, wait until you can. We have friends who put two $600 bicycles on their credit card. They rode the bikes three times in three years and were still paying off the bikes at a huge interest rate. It obviously would be better to delay a purchase and stay out of debt. Here is what the Bible says about debt: "The rich rule over the poor, and *the borrower is slave to the lender*" (Proverbs 22:7, emphasis mine). You become a slave to the lender, and debt extracts a physical and relational toll that harms relationships.

- *Spend Less Than You Make.* Spending less than you make is one of the safest spots for a marriage to be in. Drowning in debt pulls marriages apart at the seams. We suggest that if you don't have a budget, then create one today. Creating a budget and following a budget is a road map to freedom that will help your marriage in a big way.

- *Give at least 10 percent and save at least 10 percent.* This may sound like a complete oversimplification, but we don't meet many people with troubled marriages who live by this policy. Our experience is that those who save 10 percent and give 10 percent typically handle the other 80 percent in a good way as well. Not only does it show wisdom as a couple, but it takes the stress load down several notches.

Although these are financial principles, the marriages of couples who follow them will be in much better shape. As financial expert Ron Blue says, "God owns it all anyway."*

FAITH CONVERSATIONS

- How does the way we handle finances interact with our marriage relationship?
- The Bible says, "Where your treasure is, there your heart will be also" (Matthew 6:21). Is our treasure in the right place? If not, what can we do about it?
- How do we feel about our giving and savings? Do we need to make any adjustments?

*Ron and Judy Blue, *Money Matters for Parents and Their Kids* (Nashville, TN: Thomas Nelson, 1988), 47.

A STEP CLOSER

A FINANCIAL PLAN

If you aren't living by a financial plan and simple budget, then now is the time to act. Below is our adaptation of Dave Ramsey's *Seven Steps to Begin Your Journey to Financial Peace.** (We highly recommend that you read Dave's books and that you create a budget.) Read these seven steps and adapt or make goals from these to personalize your own goals. There are simple budget outlines online or in most of the helpful financial planning books available.

1. Start an emergency fund by putting away $1,000.
2. Pay off all credit card and high-interest debt and don't buy anything more on credit.
3. Place three to six months of living expenses into a savings account.
4. Give at least 10 percent and save at least 10 percent.
5. Fund as early as possible for children's college education.
6. Pay off car and home loans early.
7. Build upon your wealth and be as generous as possible.

Now create your own plan. We suggest you start with a one-year plan, a three-year plan, and a five-year plan.

*Adapted from Dave Ramsey, *Financial Peace Planner* (New York: Penguin Books, 1998), 7.

Making Your Values a Priority

And whatever you do, whether in word or deed, do it all in the name of the Lord Jesus, giving thanks to God the Father through him.

—Colossians 3:17

All couples have values. The problem is we get so caught up in the day-to-day problems of life that we don't have the time or energy to think much about our values. It's hard enough to make it till the weekend, let alone develop and then live out our priorities according to our values. However, we have seen couples and families transformed by writing out their values, posting them, and periodically looking back at those key standards that they want to live out daily. We have a Burns Family Constitution on our refrigerator. When our kids were younger, we came up with it together. It is made up of the ideals we want to live by.

Recently in a small group, we re-created our own personal values and values as a couple through dialoging and then writing them out. It was incredibly inspiring as well to see the values other people have chosen. In many ways it is like a mission statement. Your values drive your daily decisions in life, marriage, and family.

For example, the statement of our good friends Terry and Sharon looks like this: "Our mission is to develop and maintain harmonious relationships with God, each other, family, and friends." They also wrote how they would accomplish their mission. One couple took seven topics and wrote values along with these priorities: God, Spouse, Family, Work, Friends, Ministry, and Me. When you have taken the time to write out your values and share them with your spouse, there is a built-in accountability with each other as well as a closeness that transpires.

Here are Jim's thirteen values:

1. Serve God diligently and enjoy Him forever.
2. Focus on my family, giving them priority: Cathy, children (and extended family to a lesser degree).
3. Be true to my calling in ministry.
4. Be a person of integrity and a steward of the gifts God has given me with time, talent, and treasure.
5. Seek wise counsel. "Where there is no counsel, the people fall; but in the multitude of counselors there is safety" (Proverbs 11:14 NKJV).
6. Do life with honor and integrity. "The man of integrity walks securely" (Proverbs 10:9).
7. Find out where God is working and join in.

8. Treat others as if they were Jesus.
9. Take better care of my body, mind, and spirit this season.
10. Be in accountable, replenishing relationships.
11. Multiply and leverage our mission.
12. Finish well.
13. Think generationally.

We found it helpful to read other couples' values before we created our own. Now it's your turn. When Jim was in graduate school in Princeton, New Jersey, we came across many wonderful quotes by Albert Einstein, who did his life-changing work in that community. This was one of our favorites: "Try not to become a person of success, but rather a person of value."

FAITH CONVERSATIONS

- Thinking about the values we live by, how are we doing?
- Are there values from today's devotional that especially strike you as important either personally or for us as a couple?
- What values have changed for us since we were first married?

A STEP CLOSER

THE VALUES EXERCISE

As individuals, write out the top ten values you would like to live your life by. Share those values with your spouse. Now come up with five values you can establish as a couple.

God Isn't Finished With You Yet

Being confident of this, that he who began a good work in you will carry it on to completion until the day of Christ Jesus.

—Philippians 1:6

What happens in the life of a couple between the time they take each other's hands, look into each other's eyes, and declare their lifelong love, and the tougher season in the relationship that inevitably comes? Between the blissful wedding day and the stale relationship that makes them wonder if the commitment is still worth it? Let's be honest, most couples have had those days when either privately or verbally they wonder if it is all worth their while. Is the grass really greener on the other side? Does a relationship have to be so difficult? Maybe there have been times when you wanted to run away from the pain of working to develop a closer relationship. Among the many marriages you know, there have been a lot of broken dreams and thoughts of despair. Maybe that feeling has entered your mind more than once. It has with us.

Yet we find hope in the life of a man born to a slave girl in Egypt. At three months he was left adrift in the Nile, only to be rescued by one of Pharaoh's daughters. He grew up in luxury. He had the finest of everything—all he needed or wanted at his fingertips. He was adopted into one of the richest and most influential families in the world. He had the finest education and a bright future. At age forty, he killed a man. Afraid he would be found out, he fled for his life. He ended up losing his dreams and his relationships. We find this man with a new identity far away from the limelight, tending his father-in-law's sheep. He went from dining with heads of state to counting heads of sheep.

Then something pretty incredible happened. God showed up and told him He was not finished with him yet. God told Moses that He had an important job for him. The new calling was to leave the sheep and lead the entire nation of Israel out of slavery to a new "promised land." Moses argued with God and said, "I am not a great man! How can I go to the king and lead the Israelites out of Egypt?" God answered by promising to stay close to him throughout his new calling. Moses changed direction and found purpose even after losing his passion for living.

Max Lucado says it well: "Changing directions in life is not tragic. Losing passion in life is." The strong convictions of a close, intimate marriage relationship turn more toward a business partner relationship that focuses on getting bills paid, keeping the house clean, and making sure the kids get their homework done. We look up one day and say we don't like what we see. Moses probably felt that way when God approached him in a burning bush.

God spoke to Moses from that bush and told him He wasn't finished with him yet. He does the same for you—without the bush. In fact, He promises to complete the work He began in you at your wedding. He didn't promise it would be easy. He did promise to walk with you no matter what. You may think that your life is relegated to monotony and lack of passion. Well, think again. It doesn't have to be that way. Count on this promise: "There has never been the slightest doubt in my mind that the God who started this great work in you would keep at it and bring it to a flourishing finish on the very day Christ Jesus appears" (Philippians 1:6 THE MESSAGE). Wow, what a promise! What an offer! God wanted you to be reminded of that today.

FAITH CONVERSATIONS

- The story of Moses is a reminder that God doesn't give up on us. How does this story relate to our marriage today?
- If you were face-to-face with God, and He reminded you that He began a good work in us and in our marriage and He promised to stick with us till the end, how would you feel? He does promise that to us in today's Scripture verse.
- Moses must have had some regrets. In order to obey God, he needed to relinquish those regrets. Are there any regrets in our marriage that we need to relinquish to God?

A STEP CLOSER

YOUR BURNING BUSH

Imagine that you are together on a nature walk and you come across a burning bush. You remove your shoes and wait for God to speak to you as a couple. With pen and paper in hand, together come up with what you believe He would say to you. (If you need some inspiration, read the story of Moses and the burning bush in Exodus 3:1–10.)

The Burning Bush Message to us is:

Attitudes and Thoughts

As he thinks in his heart, so is he.

—Proverbs 23:7 NKJV

So much of a marriage relationship comes down to our thoughts and attitudes about the marriage. If we acted like the person we would want to come home to, most of our conflicts would disappear. Who would have thought that the quality of life isn't determined solely by what we do or by what happens to us, but how we choose to think about it.

Fulfilled marriage relationships are not based on circumstances as much as attitudes. Mark Twain once said, "I am an old man and I have known a great many troubles, but most of them never happened." The Old Testament prophet Haggai quotes none other than the Lord himself: "Now this is what the Lord Almighty says: 'Give careful thought to your ways'" (Haggai 1:5). To bring a right attitude and right thoughts to your marriage, you have to start with yourself, not your spouse. We believe two qualities are an absolute must: kindness and understanding. Both seem easy to attain, but in reality, most marriages are starving for these qualities, especially as it pertains to how we think and act toward each other.

Kindness. It's the random acts of kindness that often make a good marriage a great marriage. It's moving beyond low-level bitterness and a what's-in-it-for-me attitude toward offering empathy, compassion, and care to your relationship. It's interesting that Paul used the word *kindness* as he discussed the topic of forgiveness, when he said, "Be kind and compassionate to one another, forgiving each other, just as in Christ God forgave you" (Ephesians 4:32). An attitude of kindness often shows your forgiveness in action. Proactively treating each other with kindness does more than almost anything else to stay connected.

Understanding. A willingness to understand each other and walk in your spouse's shoes will immediately give you a closer bond. Here is a great story that illustrates how understanding changes your attitude and thinking: A young boy lived alone with his mother and handicapped grandfather. His grandfather, even though not that old, was confined to a wheelchair, spent most of his time in bed, and had great difficulty swallowing his food. His face was badly scarred and deformed. Every day the boy was assigned the task of going into his grandfather's room and feeding him lunch. As the young boy became a teenager, he became weary of his responsibility to feed his grandfather. After a particularly difficult day of feeding him, while the boy wanted to be doing his own thing, he told his mother he was finished with this chore and burden.

The mother kindly sat her son down in the living room and told the young man it was time he learned more about his grandfather. (She had held part of the story of his disability back because the grandfather insisted she not tell the boy.) "When you were a baby, there was a fire in our house," she began. "Your father was in the basement working and he thought you were with me. I was upstairs and thought you were with your father. We both rushed outside, each thinking the other one had you. Your grandfather was visiting at the time. He was the first one to realize that you were still in the burning house. He found you, wrapped you in a blanket, and made a mad dash through the flames to safety. You were fine. Your grandfather was rushed to the hospital, suffering from second- and third-degree burns all over his body. That was the day he saved your life."

By this time the young adolescent had tears in his eyes. He changed his attitude, and with no further complaints picked up his grandfather's food and took it to his room.* When you try to understand your spouse and walk in his or her shoes, it may just bring the empathy you need to draw closer.

FAITH CONVERSATIONS

- How would you rate your attitude about our relationship?
- Can you think of a time when I offered you an extra dose of kindness? I remember when you ____________________.
- What do you wish I understood about you that has impacted your life?

A STEP CLOSER

THE HONOR JOURNAL

Marriage expert Gary Smalley has developed something he calls the Honor Journal. He says, "There is no better way to build the value of

---

*Charles Stanley, *Forgiveness* (Nashville, TN: Thomas Nelson, 1987).

your mate than to start writing a never-ending list of reasons why you believe your mate is valuable."* Gary says he has four and a half pages of reasons why his wife, Norma, is valuable. Gary adds, "This is a very important secret. If you place a high enough value upon someone, that person will usually move to justify the value."** What a gift! In the space below, you can get started with your Honor Journal, but we suggest you put this on your computer or in a regular hardcover journal. May this be the start of many pages of honoring each other.

Him	**Her**
You are valuable because	You are valuable because

*Gary Smalley, *I Promise: How Five Commitments Determine the Destiny of Your Marriage* (Franklin, TN: Integrity Publishers, 2006), 44–45.

**Smalley, *I Promise: How Five Commitments Determine the Destiny of Your Marriage*, 47.

The Pain of Anger and Freedom of Forgiveness

In your anger do not sin: Do not let the sun go down while you are still angry, and do not give the devil a foothold.

—Ephesians 4:26–27

Anger destroys relationships, but did you know that anger can heal them? Let us explain. The difference is in how anger is handled. Unresolved anger causes deep-rooted bitterness and resentment that can do major damage to any relationship. But resolved anger through forgiveness is often one of the most effective ways to restore your relationship toward intimacy.

Anger is just one letter short of the word *danger.* When turned outward, anger destroys relationships and careers. When it's turned inward—as it often is—it wreaks havoc on a person's psychological and physical health. Issues like depression, anxiety, autoimmune diseases, and lack of trust can all stem from repressed anger. Some would even say anger turned inward can cause cancer and heart disease. A chiropractor told us, "All day long I work on bad backs and sore necks. Many of them are caused by accidents, but most are caused by stress and unhealthy anger."

If you remain angry with your spouse, you lose the ability to walk in the light of God and thus the ability to know and experience the love of God. Extremely angry people seem to be spiritually blind and unable to draw near to God. Winston Churchill once said, "A man is about as big as the things that make him angry." Handling the powerful emotion of anger in a healthy way will no doubt be a determining factor in your marital relationship. Our friend Gary Chapman, in his outstanding book on the subject of anger, presents five steps to handle what he calls "valid anger":

1. Consciously acknowledge to yourself that you are angry. This will make you aware that you are in touch with what is making you angry.

2. Restrain your immediate response. Here is where we need to avoid the common destructive response of speaking before we consider the damage it might do to the other person. It was Will Rogers who said, "People who fly into rage always make a bad landing."

3. Locate the focus of your anger. What exactly was it that brought this on? Often anger is fed by feelings of disappointment, hurt, rejection, and embarrassment.

4. Analyze your options. It is always better to decide ahead of time if your anger response will be healthy or harmful.

5. Take constructive action. Should you confront in love or let it go? Deciding how you will respond to your anger is always better than being spontaneous with your anger.*

Notice that today's Scripture says, "In your anger do not sin." Anger is not the sin; it's what we do with the anger that can turn it into sin. One of the great proverbs reminds us, "Fools vent their anger, but the wise quietly hold it back" (Proverbs 29:11 NLT). We find that connection and intimacy are found when we can honestly and openly share with each other our anger, fear, resentments, and remorse, as well as our forgiveness and appreciation. Before there is freedom in a relationship, there is often pain. Take the high road; face your anger, pain, and fear in order to find forgiveness and freedom, which always draw a couple together.

FAITH CONVERSATION

- How has unhealthy anger hurt our relationship?
- Some people repress their anger while others let it out. How do we deal with anger?
- How could we better process anger, keeping in mind these verses:

  "Fools vent their anger, but the wise quietly hold it back" (Proverbs 29:11 NLT).

  "In your anger do not sin: Do not let the sun go down while you are still angry, and do not give the devil a foothold" (Ephesians 4:26).

---

*Gary Chapman, *Anger: Handling a Powerful Emotion in a Healthy Way* (Chicago: Northfield Publishing, 2007), adapted from page 35.

A STEP CLOSER

BEFORE FREEDOM, COMES PAIN

We have found the statements below with the fill-in-the-blanks extremely helpful for bringing about a healthy conversation. Some have called this the "stages of truth." We prefer to say, "Before freedom, comes pain." The purpose of this experience is not to dump your anger on your spouse, but rather to talk about the issues so that you can overcome your anger and resentment.

Fill in the blanks on your own. When you are both finished, have one person at a time answer all the questions without comment from the other. When you are both finished, then you can dialogue about it. Make sure you have scheduled enough quality time to give this powerful experience the investment you need to complete it.

Anger and Resentment

I'm angry that ______________________________

I resent ______________________________

I don't like it when ______________________________

Hurt

It hurts me when ______________________________

I feel sad when ______________________________

I feel disappointed about ______________________________

Fear

I am afraid that ______________________________

I feel scared when ______________________________

I'm afraid of you when ______________________________

Remorse and Accountability

I'm sorry that______________________________________

I didn't mean to ____________________________________

Please forgive me for ________________________________

Forgiveness and Appreciation

I forgive you for ____________________________________

I love you because __________________________________

Thank you for ______________________________________

Learning to Apologize

Therefore confess your sins to each other and pray for each other so that you may be healed.

—James 5:16

The positive strength of a heartfelt apology is one of the most powerful ways to draw closer and experience true forgiveness. Couples do have an incredible capacity to forgive. But without a genuine apology, it is much more difficult.

Our heavenly Father is the ultimate One to show us how to forgive. He chose to send his own Son to be the sacrifice for the forgiveness of our sins. "He so loved the world that he gave his Son." Those are powerful words of unmerited favor and severe mercy. Apologies come in all shapes and sizes. You might bump into someone in the mall and say something like, "Excuse me, I'm sorry," or devastate your spouse with words or actions and through tears of repentance have to say something like, "I am so sorry. Will you please forgive me?"

In many situations we are pulled between the longing for justice and a desire for mercy. There have been many times when we have wondered if the people involved in broken relationships would have only made a sincere apology for their actions, would they still be in the mess they are in. Gary Chapman in his book *The Five Languages of Apology** teaches us five separate types of apology. All five are important and need to be used at different times. They all need to be sincere and heartfelt or eventually the apology will backfire.

1. *I am sorry.* This is a simple expression of regret. Just admitting your regret may be all the other person needs.

2. *I was wrong.* You accept responsibility for your actions. Being defensive and making excuses will not take you where you want to go, but accepting your part in it does wonders for connection.

3. *What can I do to make it right?* Sometimes in an apology there needs to be some form of making restitution. If you have wronged someone, they may need you to do the right thing by taking care of the issue. When people steal from someone, they need to apologize and make it right.

4. *I will try not to do that again.* This type of an apology is genuine repentance. The word *repentance* means you were moving in one direction and now you will turn around and do the right thing.

5. *Will you please forgive me?* This is an act of requesting forgiveness. When you admit you have broken your word to your spouse, ask for forgiveness and receive it; this is one of the most freeing

---

*Gary Chapman and Jennifer Thomas, *The Five Languages of Apology* (Chicago: Northfield Publishing, 2006).

experiences. It is quite similar to the unfailing, unconditional love and forgiveness God bestows upon us.

One night David looked from his porch and watched another man's wife bathing. Lust burned in his heart, and the king of Israel ended up not only committing adultery but having the woman's husband killed. It was not the best moment for David. In fact, he deserved death. We see the amazing love of God through the apology David makes to his Lord concerning his sin. We can learn something from David in how to apologize to our spouse. In a way, he uses all five types of apology mentioned in the list above. More important, he was sincere. David says in his psalm of apology and confession: "Have mercy on me, O God, according to your unfailing love; according to your great compassion. . . . Wash away all my iniquity and cleanse me from my sin. . . . Cleanse me with hyssop, and I will be clean; wash me, and I will be whiter than snow. Let me hear joy and gladness; let the bones you have crushed rejoice. Create in me a pure heart, O God, and renew a steadfast spirit within me" (taken from Psalm 51). You see the heart of David in his plea to God. No one would condone his actions. He did what he needed to do. He expressed his regret, accepted his responsibility, promised to make restitution where he could, was genuinely repentant, and asked for forgiveness. What God wants to see from us as we apologize to each other is similar to what was required of David. True forgiveness follows an authentic apology.

FAITH CONVERSATIONS

- Is there a type of apology that is hard for you to offer? Is there a type that is harder for you to receive?

- Have you ever felt a bit like David as expressed in this Psalm?
- How would you finish the sentence "When I apologize to you, I feel ____."

A STEP CLOSER

A HEARTFELT APOLOGY

No marriage is offense free. Two sinful people living together have lots of opportunity for heartfelt apology. Take some time to pray and decide if there is something you have done or said to your spouse that begs an apology. If you have something on your heart, offer that sincere apology to your spouse right away. Close in a time of prayer, and if something was stirred up in either of you that you feel needs some help to resolve, seek the advice of a wise counselor.

JIM and CATHY BURNS have been married for over thirty years. They have the privilege to speak to couples each year through conferences on "Creating an Intimate Relationship" and "Growing Together Spiritually." Jim and Cathy founded the ministry HomeWord in 1985 with the goal of bringing help and hope to struggling families. Cathy is a teacher at a Christian school for kids with learning disabilities. Jim is host of the *HomeWord* radio broadcasts heard daily in over 800 communities and is senior director of the HomeWord Center for Youth and Family at Azusa Pacific University. Jim and Cathy's passion is to build God-honoring families through communicating practical Christian faith.

In addition to the radio program and their seminars and conferences, Jim is an award-winning author whose books include *Creating an Intimate Marriage, The 10 Building Blocks for a Healthy Family,* and *Confident Parenting.*

Jim and Cathy have three grown daughters and live in Southern California.

HOME HW WORD

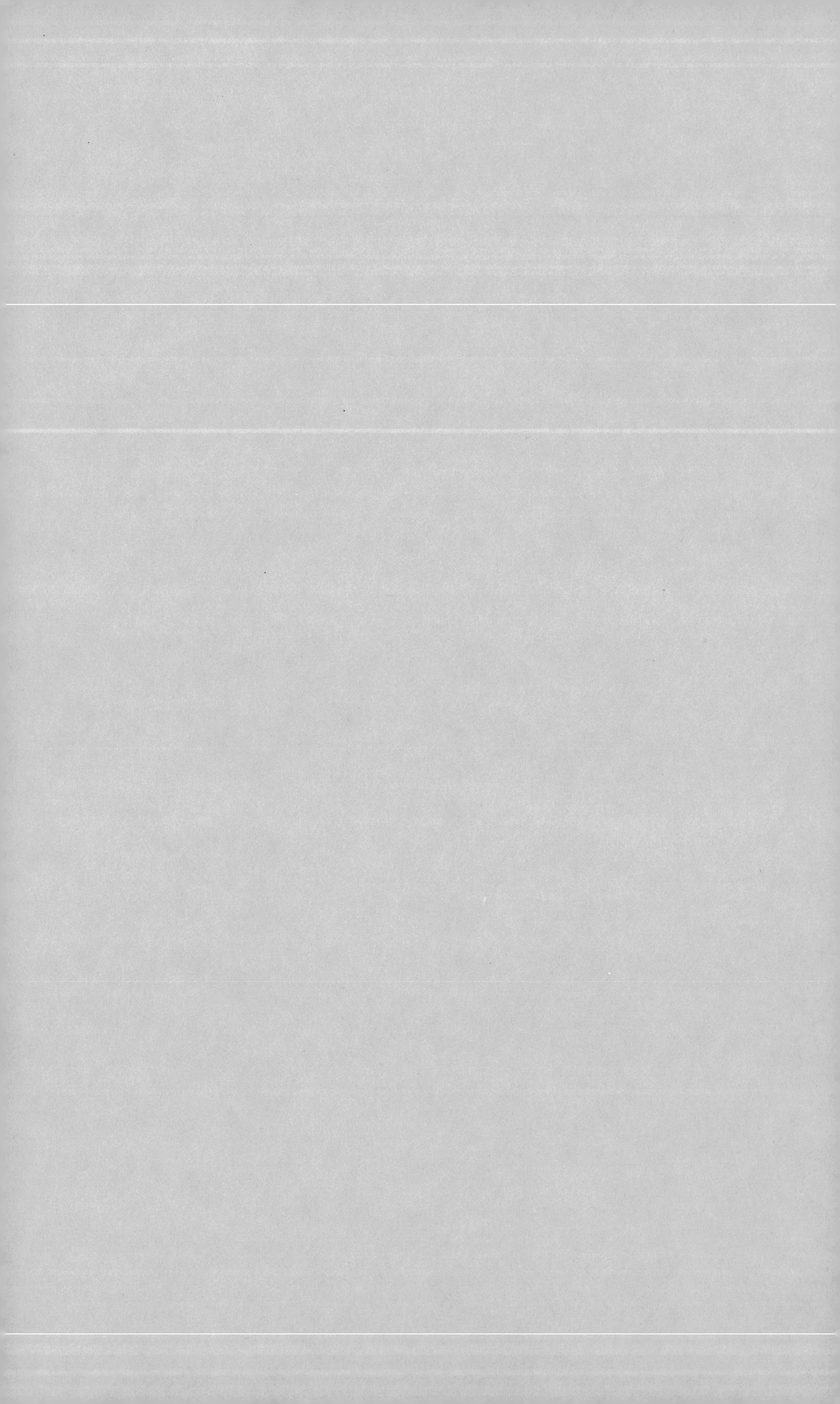